THALES PANAGIDES

Odyssey to the Heart

To my mom who taught me how to love, my dad who taught me to believe, my uncle Stahis who taught me to view the world with an open heart and mind, and my beloved wife and daughters who teach me daily on our life journey together.

Contents

One

Slow and Less

She wasn't wearing any makeup, as far as I could tell, and was as beautiful as nature intended her to be. She seemed friendly and wise beyond her years, the type of person who'd know exactly which train I should take. She exemplified, in my eyes, the definition of purity and elegance. She wore a pretty sun hat that matched her flowing white dress. Something about her set her apart from the other commuters at the station. For one, she wasn't in a rush. She stood still, holding two books in her hand.

I'll never forget that chance encounter because her guidance set me on a path that led to inner peace and a zest for life I didn't know existed. Life before our encounter had included a series of broken relationships, financial anxiety and a time bomb of health issues that was about to explode any minute. The company to which I had dedicated thirty-five years of my life was closing down and the savings I had accumulated were invested with a businessman who turned out to be a fraudster. My marriage of twenty years had produced two beloved children but ended in a bitter divorce. I needed help and, as fate would have it, she appeared unexpectedly with guidance that would change my life forever. I was nervous about approaching her but felt at ease the moment she turned to me with a twinkle in her eye and a bright smile on her face.

"You're lost, aren't you?" she said.

I nodded.

"Excuse me," I said, a little confused. "Do you know which train I should take in order to acquire the same sense of peace and grace you clearly project?"

She rolled her eyes and, in a soft voice, said, "My dear, that train's available to anybody who surrenders to their heart."

"Surrenders to their heart?" I repeated curiously.

She giggled. "Yes. It's a feeling I hope you'll come to experience one day."

I nodded and pulled out the ticket stub from my previous train ride.

She recognized it instantly. "Looks like you were on the 'fast and more' train," she said.

I nodded.

She assured me I wouldn't have to purchase another ticket for the remaining part of my journey and told me to pursue a life path that wasn't as fast as the previous train I was on. I was still confused but figured that "slow and less" could symbolize the direction my life would be taking.

"Is that all?" I asked with a bit of trepidation.

"One more thing," she added. "Tell me what you see when you look into my eyes."

I hadn't expected to hear that but I went ahead and gazed into her eyes. Time seemed to dissolve into eternity. I felt an overwhelming sense of serenity. To my surprise, I heard myself saying, "Beauty."

She smiled and said, "Just know that when your heart begins to see beyond the reach of your eyes, your life will change forever."

I wondered what she meant but didn't ask and, instead, just said, "Thank you."

Suddenly she was gone. I waited patiently on the crowded platform as various trains arrived and departed. Eventually, I decided to take a chance and board the train that had just arrived in the station, no matter where it was going. It stood out from most of the others I had taken in my life. It seemed to move slower and didn't make as much noise. Yellowish with unusually large windows, it didn't look as modern as the other trains. I was intrigued and didn't hesitate for a moment to board it.

I was carrying a small handbag with a few essentials: reading glasses, a bottle of water, and two notepads. As I climbed on board, I was greeted by a friendly lady who evidently worked on the train. You could tell that she absolutely loved her job.

"Welcome," she said with a beautiful smile. "I have the perfect compartment for you."

I knew I was in good hands and followed her down the spacious and well-lit corridor. As she walked, she seemed to be dancing. Some people have musical personalities and she was clearly one of them. We arrived at the end of the corridor and she pointed to my compartment on the left-hand side.

"Here it is," she said. "Enjoy the trip."

I entered and was astonished. That part of the carriage had ten comfortable tanned seats positioned around a thick wooden table. The seats could be adjusted to recline and rotate. It was an unusual layout but one that encouraged passengers to interact with each other. There were four other seats, one in each corner of the compartment, for passengers who wanted a little more privacy.

I already knew that this trip was going to be different. This time I intended to savor the journey and keep a diary of everything I heard and saw. I settled into the seat beside the window, took a sip from my water bottle and proceeded to pull out my notepad. Across the top of the blank page I wrote, "Slow and Less." As I did on every trip, I thought of my mother, who, at the beginning of every journey, would pinch three fingers, as chefs do when sprinkling salt over food, and make the sign of the cross three times. It was a silent gesture of gratitude, one I knew that would also keep me safe on my own journey if I kept the faith.

As I settled down, I looked around and noticed that everyone seemed visibly happier than the stressed-out passengers on the express trains I had been traveling on throughout most of my adult life. They emanated an upbeat aura, a positive energy which reaffirmed that I was heading in the right direction. I sighed as my thoughts flashed back to one particular day in my childhood. It was one of those recurring memories of the time when I was a carefree teenager, basking in the sun on a beach nestled between white majestic cliffs and a calm blue ocean, a playground fit for kings and queens, who were known to have actually frequented that very spot thousands of years ago. In fact, remnants of their lives were still visible as ancient castle ruins not far from the beach. I remember how being there was the closest thing to pure bliss that I had ever experienced. Only one thing could complete it: ice cream!

I was in luck. A friend's father happened to pull up in a pink and blue ice cream van. He owned an ice cream factory and spent long summer afternoons trawling the beach, handing out scoops of joy to the children and adults scattered along the shoreline. We exchanged pleasantries while he prepared my favorite flavor: a double scoop of dark chocolate. I thanked him and savored each lick before the ice cream had a chance to melt down my fingers. Finally, all that was left was the crown jewel: the tip of the cone. It was delicious. I was so caught up in my treat that I didn't realize that the ice cream man was still standing there.

His voice startled me, as did what he said: "Young man, enjoy it because life ends as quickly as an ice cream."

For some reason, those words struck a chord I have never got out of my head. Decades have passed since that unforgettable summer day but it feels like yesterday. I'd hear the ice cream man's words over and over again throughout my life. Anyone over the age of fifty seemed to be telling me, in his or her own way, to be grateful and appreciate every moment as if it were the last one.

I wasn't aware of it on that brilliant summer day but time has a way of catching up and leaving random clues along the way. It can be a wrinkle that appears on your forehead or your precious daughter starting to go on dates. As the train began to move, I caught myself thinking about the transient nature of life and wondered how it could serve as a wake-up call, a reminder to appreciate every moment, including the difficult ones we face. I knew that life was no easy ride but I was determined to make the best of this trip. I grabbed my pen and wrote that I wanted it, as a new chapter in my life, to lead to personal growth, self-discovery and spiritual awareness.

Two

The Well

My thoughts were interrupted by a tall, slim gentleman sitting across from me.

"Is that an Express ticket?" he asked, glancing at the ticket placed between two of the pages of my journal.

He wore sunglasses, a white polo shirt and dark blue jeans. He was sandwiched between two little girls, probably his daughters. I glanced around but couldn't spot their mother. All three of them were facing me. The only thing that separated us was the wooden table and my curiosity.

I nodded in answer to the man's question, wondering how he could possibly know I had an Express ticket.

"I used to have one of those but gave it up after losing my wife, job and home."

In a strange kind of way, it was reassuring to know I wasn't the only one who had faced some difficult times in life. I told him how sorry I was to hear that.

"Yeah. It was the most difficult time of my life. Those events, coming one after the other, brought me to my knees. It's kind of strange but they sparked my spiritual awakening."

I leaned in, anxious to hear more.

"You see, I hurt a lot of people. I didn't pay attention to the things that truly mattered in life, like my family and friends. I was on a destructive path, not caring about anything or anybody other than myself. It took a crisis to wake me up."

"How's that?" I asked.

"Well, on one particular day, for no apparent reason, I visited a cemetery. I walked for about half an hour before sitting down on a wooden bench. Not far from where I sat was a funeral gathering. A minister was presiding over a burial and, as I looked at the handful of people attending, I realized that they were my own family and friends. "Who died?" I wondered, in a panic. Then it dawned on me that the funeral was mine.

"I yelled, 'Hey I'm not dead! I'm here! I'm alive! Stop what you're doing! Can't you hear me, damn it?" I pleaded at the top of my lungs for them to look at me and told them how sorry I was for everything I had done. I shouted over and over again but nobody could hear me.

"And that's when I began to sob uncontrollably. After a while, an elderly man came and sat beside me. He put an arm around my shoulders and asked if I was okay. As soon as he did it, the emotional burden I had been carrying for years suddenly vanished and was replaced with a sense of calm. It's hard to explain. I just have to tell you that, on my quest to find something rich and fulfilling, I ended up discovering that all I ever needed was inside me. I realized it was something everybody possessed and could harness, no matter what their circumstances were. I've heard people describe such experiences as a kind of shift or awakening and I think that's what this was."

I asked him what it was that we all possessed.

"Well," he said, "if you embark on an inward journey of personal and spiritual growth, you'll end up discovering a bottomless well."

"A well?" I repeated, curious.

"Yeah, imagine uncovering a magnificent source that emanates endless joy and love. You see, I've come to realize that life reflects what's inside our well. If our well is brimming with love, then what we experience will be reflected back to us as love. Just think about it. Isn't that life-transforming?"

"Is it?" I wondered silently.

"Any negative thoughts you have diminish in the presence of love. If your emotional well consists of hate and resentment, that's all you're going to see and experience in others too. You'll constantly be suspicious of people's motives and assume that they harbor the same feelings about you. If you're the jealous type, you'll think everybody else is jealous of you too. You see, in a way, what you see in others is just a reflection of what you feel inside. You get it, don't you? It's that simple. Life's a reflection of the feelings we harbor in our well. If your well's contaminated, everything around you appears toxic."

My eyes lit up. I remembered what the elegant woman at the train station had told me earlier. I had interpreted what she said as meaning that life becomes richer and more beautiful when viewed through the lens of love or, in her words, 'through the heart'. It was all beginning to make sense. The woman at the station and the passenger across from me were referring to the same thing. They both believed that life is best experienced through love.

8

I turned my face toward the window where, instead of an open vista, I saw my reflection staring back at me. I smiled and the window smiled back. I pointed my index finger at the window and the window pointed an index finger right back at me. I frowned and the window frowned back. I was acting like a child, amused by something so simple as observing my own reflection, but I wasn't bothered by what the others in the carriage might think of a middle-aged man making gestures at the window. It didn't matter because I had realized something important. The window, like the well, was a powerful example of what the father meant when he said that life reflected the feelings we harbor inside us. I wondered how something so obvious could have escaped me. I began to scribble some notes. This time I wrote about a future where every student under the age of fifteen would be required to look into a mirror and explain how their reflection was also a metaphor for how he or she lived and perceived life. I marveled at how our world, just like the train's window, reflects how we feel inside. I ordered a cup of coffee and continued to write: "Experience the world, not only through your wonderful and ever-so-powerful senses but also with your heart." I leaned back in my reclining seat and reflected on what I thought was the greatest discovery in the world.

Three

Empathy

I must have dozed off because the next thing I knew, I had woken up to the girls arguing over something. Their father apologized for the lively exchange while I tried to figure out what was going on. They appeared to be drawing random letters of the alphabet and one was accusing the other of not drawing the letter they had agreed on. I noticed a pile of papers scattered on the table, each piece with a big letter sketched on it. But they weren't just letters; they were colorful and cute, as you would expect from any child. They were playing to see who could draw the best letter M and then they would ask their father to choose. The younger girl, sitting directly across from her sister, teased the older one for not knowing the correct letters of the alphabet.

"We agreed to draw M, not W," said the little one.

Of course, they had both drawn an M but, from her vantage point, each was seeing a W on the other's page.

I watched the girls quarrel until their father intervened and asked them to settle down. He told them to stand up and trade places. As they switched and changed seats, they were puzzled but then they realized what had happened.

"Sweeties," said the father, "see how we can be wrong and still think we're right?"

The girls giggled and seemed a little embarrassed.

I thought about how my life would have turned out better if I hadn't been so quick to judge or impose my beliefs on others without first trying to understand their point of view or where they were coming from.

"Girls," continued their father, "I want to teach you an important word. It's called 'empathize.'"

The little one repeated the word out loud and asked what it meant.

"'Empathize' means trying to understand and share the feelings of others. Consider it a game, because you get to imagine what it would be like if you were someone else, just like actors do when they take on a role in a play."

The little one thought it sounded a lot like the game of 'pretend' they often played.

"So, girls, as you grow up and become adults, try to empathize with everybody as much as you can."

I knew the girls didn't fully understand what he meant but I did. Empathy was a quality I had lacked for many years.

As the little one stood up, she flung her arms across the top of the table and accidentally knocked over my paper cup that was full of coffee. It fell to the ground and made a mess of the floor. The little girl was shaken and began to cry.

"It's okay. Don't cry. It's only a paper cup," I said reassuringly. "Do you think the cup's crying?" I asked with a cheeky smile.

"No," she said, trying to catch her breath and wipe her tears away.

"Good, so let's make a deal. Let's agree never to cry over things that don't cry for us." She nodded approvingly as we high-fived each other. The father smiled, "Did you hear that girls? Don't cry over things that don't cry for you."

It was a great lesson for the girls and for me too – I used to place a lot more importance on material things than on people.

Four

The Greatest Show on Earth

The girls' father and I continued to chat. He told me about a life-changing encounter he had had with a fisherman several years before. He said the fisherman had given him an education in life that he had never acquired in decades of schooling. Eager to know more, I asked him what it was.

"I went on a business trip to close an important deal for my firm and was away for weeks. The girls kept calling and I promised to go home as soon as the negotiations were concluded."

I felt a tight feeling in my gut when he said he promised the girls he'd return. I thought of the promises I had made but didn't keep.

He continued: "One day, I left a meeting feeling optimistic that we were close to reaching a deal. I decided to take a break from work and stepped out of the client's luxurious beachfront office and took a stroll along the promenade. I felt uncomfortable in my stuffy business suit and loosened my tie, something I hated having to wear. I could see and hear the signs of summer everywhere. The sun was beaming while children lined up to buy ice cream beneath the shade of a tall palm tree. It brought back memories of the idyllic pictures my friends would share from their trips to the Caribbean."

I knew exactly what he was talking about, having spent some of the happiest days of my life on a beach.

"I walked to the end of the pier," my new friend continued, "and approached a shirtless, tanned fisherman sporting a scruffy beard. I introduced myself and the first thing I asked was how many fish he had caught."

"'Sir,' he said, 'I didn't catch any fish and it doesn't matter.'

"'But why?' I asked curiously.

"'Because I catch something bigger than fish.'

"'Like what?' I asked with a dose of sarcasm.

"'I catch the most spectacular show on planet earth. I have caught 23,000 sunrises from the east and a heap more sunsets from the west.'

"I could hardly believe it; that amounted to sixty-three years of honoring the Universe's gift to us while I couldn't recall seeing more than a dozen sunrises in my entire life. I felt like a fool as I thought of all the magnificent shows I had missed out on over the years. But at the same time, I felt encouraged, knowing the price of admission was simply being aware they existed."

His story gave me a jolt, like an alarm clock in the early morning.

The girls' father went on to say that the fisherman had told him about a rich friend who had questioned his obsession with fishing and thought he was wasting his time. Without hesitating, the dedicated fisherman told his friend, "Buddy, you've got a lot of money and I have a lot of time. So let me ask you, who's the richer?"

The fisherman's wealthy friend was lost for words and realized that time was, indeed, one of the best gifts he could give himself, one that all the money in the world couldn't buy. Ever since that day, the man never questioned the fisherman's intentions and often showed up to watch the greatest show on earth with his wise friend.

Five

Beyond "Why"

"Can I ask you something personal?" I asked the girls' father.

"Sure," he said, "my life's an open book."

"How did you lose your wife?"

"Cancer came knocking on her door or, should I say, our family's door. She never answered, hoping it'd go away, but it had other plans. The worst you could imagine. It charged straight into the temple of her body and began helping itself to the bounties of her life. It caused destruction and sapped energy out of everything she ever was. She was furious and I was scared.

"'Get out. Leave us alone,' I'd yell aimlessly. I started feeling guilty and blaming myself for the stress in our relationship. My extended absences from home and last-minute business trips were a constant source of tension in our marriage. More than anything, my wife was worried about our girls growing up without a mother. We had so many questions but very few answers. We didn't know what had caused her illness. We thought of all the things we might have done differently that could have prevented her fatal encounter with cancer. We wept in silence.

"I remember asking the universe all sorts of questions like 'Why her? Why us? Why now?' I demanded a response but never got one. I wondered how cancer could have violated our family's life and had the audacity not to explain why. I was furious.

"I took some time off work to stay home and support my wife. As soon as our girls left for school in the morning, my wife would skip breakfast and head straight into our bedroom. It was her sanctuary. She didn't feel like socializing and preferred to spend time alone. The house felt eerily quiet. Sometimes I'd tiptoe to her closed door and peek through the keyhole to see if she was okay. I remember seeing her clasping her pale hands against her chest and bowing her head while a jasmine incense candle flickered on the table in front of her. I assumed she was praying or meditating.

"Hope was fading and so was my faith. Bills started piling up and we started missing payments on our mortgage. As the weeks became months and we entered the first year, I didn't want to believe what my eyes could clearly see. Cancer was taking a huge toll on her body. She was beginning to look frail and yet, despite her failing health, we still believed in miracles. We had heard they can happen. But any glimpse of hope we once had was beginning to slip away with each visit to the hospital. The cancer insisted on spreading its presence and becoming a permanent resident. My wife gradually slipped into depression, lost a lot of weight and had no interest in doing anything. I couldn't allow her to give up but, as winter turned to spring and spring into summer, she started talking about accepting her fate and feeling, in an odd way, better for doing so. It seemed like a paradox – as things in life often are – that surrendering to cancer had given her a sense of peace and an outlook on life that she had not had in years. She said it felt as if a tremendous weight had been lifted off her and she even joked about feeling so light she could fly. I wasn't amused.

"A few hours before she passed away, she insisted she'd be fine and told me to make sure I looked after our precious girls. I'd often heard her say, 'Life's what it is, and the sooner we accept that, the better we are.'

"I didn't understand what she meant but I think it was her way of coping with the constant pain she had to endure. She had no choice. The alternative would have been to muster whatever strength she had left to battle the inevitable. I admired her ability to transcend a billion cells attacking her body. There's no way I would've been able to cope with the suffering my wife endured with such grace and dignity, qualities that cancer couldn't extinguish.

"I held her head close to mine as she whispered into my ear, 'The healing begins when your heart accepts what is and is able to get past 'Why?''

"Those were the last words that came out of her mouth. Her eyes closed and, in some mysterious way, I knew everything would be all right. I understood that grieving would be part of the healing process but so would moving beyond why this had happened to our family. That's what she wanted from me and that's what I did. She'd speak of dealing with pain as having some type of higher purpose. Can you believe that? I sure didn't back then but I do now.

"You've got to accept that suffering and grieving are part

of the human experience. It happens, sooner or later, to everybody. Some people become bitter while others come out of the experience feeling blessed and aware, more than ever before, that life's a sacred gift to be appreciated every second of the day. Your job is to arrive at this awareness and not let it go to waste, which is what most people do. I'm living proof that inner peace arises from acceptance but it's got to be unconditional acceptance. It's one of life's most powerful remedies and it doesn't cost a thing. It clears your mind and soothes your soul. Trust me, it feels good."

I thought how it had to be true. After all, this was a man who had lost his wife to cancer and had gone through so much, yet he seemed to have overcome it all and, in the process, become a more present and loving father to his children – something which he confessed to not having been in the past.

I thanked him for sharing his personal story and noted in my journal, "Healing begins when your heart accepts what is, and moves beyond 'Why?'"

Six

Awareness

We were traveling alongside a picturesque creek when I noticed a raft of ducks being fed by a kayaker. At one point, he extended his right arm to the sky with the palm of his hand spread wide open. Blackbirds swarmed above and took turns at snatching small pieces of bread from the kayaker's hand. The contrast of blackbirds hovering in the clear blue sky and white ducks being fed pieces of bread from the hands of a kayaker was one of the most spectacular things I had ever seen. The strange thing is that I felt I had experienced this before. I wasn't sure if I had witnessed it in a dream or had actually experienced it while traveling through life on the "fast and more" train.

The uncertainty bothered me. Thoughts of the fisherman's story came to my mind. Here I was witnessing one of those great shows the fisherman was talking about and yet I wasn't sure if I had actually seen it happen before now.

I vowed to pay more attention, even to things as small and

slow as a snail. I'd make an effort to enjoy where I was at any given moment and never again confuse it with a dream or past experience. I continued marveling at the ducks and blackbirds, who seemed to enjoy swimming and flying almost in unison with the kayaker.

I felt the urge to write something unrelated to the kayaker. I'm not sure why but this is what came out: "Wild gardens aren't an assortment of plants and flowers to be profited from, but an orchestra of life to be enjoyed by all. Trust that a day will arrive when you're graced with the ability to hear and enjoy the orchestra in everything that is life. You'll know when this happens. It's when you enjoy the sight and smell of a flower so much that instead of picking it, you let it be where it was meant to be. It's when you begin to see, feel or hear something so beautiful, you shed tears of joy and gratitude for bearing witness to it. When that begins to happen, suddenly everything in life becomes a gift wrapped for you. Everything."

Seven

Ripples

The next thing I knew, the train had come to a sudden halt and all the passengers were being asked to disembark. Apparently there was a mechanical fault that had to be repaired. Some passengers sighed, others mumbled and a young woman in her 20s could be heard complaining out loud.

The girls' father said, "Poor thing, she must have caught the wrong train. Can someone remind her that this one is pretty slow and old?"

We laughed when we heard him say that but I noticed a lot of people appeared a little scared about what had just happened. As we climbed down from the train and walked into an open field, we could still hear the young woman venting her frustration over the unexpected stop.

I was also upset but tried to conceal it from my new friend. He noticed me grimace and asked how I felt. I admitted that the unplanned stop was stressing me out. I told him we could be stuck for hours and maybe even days. He appreciated my openness and suggested we go for a walk. Within minutes, we came across a still pond and decided to sit down while his daughters played tag on the other side.

He looked toward his girls and asked me to pay attention. He wanted to demonstrate something because, as he said, "We forget what we hear but remember what we see."

He proceeded to place an egg-shaped stone in the palm of my hand and instructed me to throw it into the water. I took a step back and threw the rock as far as I could. It landed spot in the center of the pond.

I felt a friendly pat on my back.

"Great throw," said the man. "Keep your eyes on the ripples and follow each one to its conclusion."

I did. Dozens of ripples travelled methodically over the surface of the water until they embraced the edge of the pond.

"Now imagine you were the stone and each ripple a spoken word or deed. What you say or do has the potential to affect everybody around you and, when it does, everybody around them. And that's why what you say and do matters. Just like ripples impacting the entire pond, your actions affect people. What you do and say have the potential to inspire or shatter dreams."

I thanked him for the vivid analogy and assured him I had got the message. I then asked him what we could do to avoid or control negative ripples, such as those from the young woman who had been complaining earlier on.

"Good question," he said. "First of all, we have to admit that we can't control what other people say and do. It's an illusion to think we can and I can't imagine you'd want to be a dictator," he said teasingly. "Our desire to control events, even with the best intentions, is the cause of most of our problems. Right?"

I was skeptical and I tried to convince him that nothing would get done if we didn't plan for or control certain outcomes in our life.

He gave me a puzzled look and said, "Planning an event is one thing and controlling it is another thing altogether. Control means having power over someone or something but life doesn't work that way. You can plan and prepare all you want for a pleasant walk in the woods but an unexpected deadly snake can bite and kill you in less time than it takes to treat you. You can plan to visit a friend on the other side of town, only to cross the path of a stray bullet. Being in the wrong place at the wrong time isn't as uncommon as you think. Or think about when the universe unleashes its omnipotent power. Contrary to what we think, it does what it's supposed to do in the right place and at the right time. It's not a coincidence. Nothing is. Absolutely nothing. We may go to sleep at night and abruptly wake up the next minute, fearing for our lives. Who'd think we'd end up in the vicinity of a flash flood, an earthquake, a hurricane or a raging fire? In such a case, if you're one of the lucky ones, you'll wake up the next morning to see your house intact but sadly discover that your neighbors weren't so fortunate. They lost their home, which was mortgaged for thirty years, gone with the wind or engulfed in flames with nothing to show but ashes and memories."

I thought of how my friend had lost his wife to cancer and yet, despite everything, managed to move on and be strong for his daughters. I also thought of how surrendering to adverse situations, though not easy, was perhaps one of the key ingredients for healing and moving on in life. Struggles are a certainty and how you cope with them makes all the difference.

He continued, "We have no control over our destiny and no amount of planning can prevent certain events from happening. Having gone through a series of close calls, I've come to believe that our 'expiry date' is predetermined the day we're born."

It was an interesting point of view and one I was willing to consider. I continued to listen.

"And now the good news," he said. "We can control how we react to people and events. It's an acquired skill that takes time to master, but once you do, you'll notice things changing for the better. Think about it. Your need to control a situation is the reason why you and the young lady who was complaining feel stress. It happens when things don't go our way. This dissonance, or gap between what we want and what actually happens, serves no purpose other than to cause friction in our lives."

I knew exactly what he was talking about. I thought of the times when things hadn't gone my way and how frustrated and anxious I had felt.

"Think of all the people you know who live their lives obsessed with imaginary ripples that are negatively charged, ripples that were created in the past but continue to occupy people's minds and affect their well-being. It's sad. Spectacular sandcastles are constantly being destroyed over things that were said or done years ago, and over things that might never even occur in the future."

"I get it, but how do I prevent negative thoughts, or ripples as you said, from entering my mind and affecting how I feel?"

"The answer lies within, my friend. Let me explain. Enlightened souls tell us we should be the change we wish to see in the world, while the ancient philosophers implored us to 'know ourselves.' These are powerful messages and they help answer your question by pointing to an inward journey where the world is viewed through the lens of a loving heart."

I was still confused.

He asked me to imagine our senses reacting to things on the surface of the water.

"When a ripple crosses our path, like something we hear or see, it affects how we feel, but not if observed from the stillness present at the bottom of the pond."

I was beginning to understand.

"Just think how calm life is on the floor of the deepest oceans in the world, despite the turbulence on the surface of the water caused by crossing ships and storms. To access this calm space, you have to travel inwards, towards your heart where a sense of inner peace and love reside. Got it?"

I nodded.

"Again, one of the best ways to cope with the ripples in your life is not to try to divert or control them but to receive them on a deeper level. When you begin to view the world through the lens of love and empathy, ripples no longer affect how you feel and, in turn, how you think. Love's a natural antidote, a powerful immunity against the negative ripples in your life."

I remembered a note I had made in my journal: "See the world with your heart and not just with your eyes."

I wrote, "Inner peace is found within."

I thanked him for sharing these thoughts with me and asked him another question that was on my mind, this time about the people who, deliberately or unintentionally, create negative ripples. "Sometimes the things they say and do upset me, so I'm curious to know if their behavior also affects them?"

He said, "Open your ears and listen carefully."

He raised his voice and yelled out to his girls, "I Love You!"

The girls acknowledged their father and cheerfully waved back. The universe reciprocated and echoed back, "I Love You."

"Have you ever thought that everything in life, including the things we can't see, vibrates with a certain type of energy?"

I nodded.

"The energy we put out into the world comes back to us sooner or later. It's amazing. It flows as if being guided by an invisible hand, a higher intelligence."

I asked him if this was what was meant by karma or cause and effect.

"In a way, yes. Our actions, such as when you threw the stone into the water or my shouting out 'I Love You' to the girls, created a form of energy in motion. When released into the universe, it can influence a person's life in a negative or positive way. It's a form of karmic frequency."

I asked him to elaborate.

"Well," he said. "Energy is in constant flux and, at some point, revisits the person as if to say, 'Hey, remember me?' It can express itself differently from when it was first released into the universe but the charge remains the same." I remembered my mother's words: "Life's like a wheel; what goes around comes around."

I thanked my friend and wondered if our encounter had been pure coincidence or karma in action. I wasn't sure but everything was beginning to make sense and become as clear as my reflection in the pond. I was happy and so was my reflection.

***

I looked up to see the face of the girls' father beaming with contentment.

"Isn't this moment priceless?" he asked, pointing to his daughters who were dancing and giggling in the lush, fragrant field across the pond. "Cherish it. Take it in. Do you realize how fortunate we are to be alive and witnessing this moment? If the train hadn't broken down, we wouldn't have experienced this wonderful sight. It's a perfect example of what it means to see the beauty in everything, no matter what our circumstances are. Do you see how every moment exists for a reason, to teach us something about ourselves and life?"

I nodded in agreement and told him how fascinated I was by everything he said.

"Aren't we all, after all, just students enrolled in a class called 'Moments?' We attend but pay little attention to the lessons each moment provides. Are you with me or still worried about the train, and when and if it will ever be fixed?"

I assured him I was paying attention.

"Good," he said. "You're a great student."

Of course, I understood the importance of being present, more aware and appreciative of everything around me but it wasn't easy. My thoughts kept drifting into the future, preoccupied with things I had to do or my mind would often slip back into the past.

He sensed my uneasiness, snapped his fingers and said, "Relax, we're about to witness the greatest show on earth."

I nodded and was embarrassed to admit that the fisherman's message of gratitude had finally sunk in. The sun had begun to set on the Western horizon, as if trying to set the world on fire before its departure. For a brief moment, the sun used the sky as its canvas and produced a masterpiece, a carnival of colors with shades of violet, red and blue. I held my breath and marveled at the spectacle.

Eight

Signposts

The train conductor was approaching us. She wore casual dark green pants and a white-buttoned shirt. She looked comfortable in her uniform but what caught my attention were the patterned turtles stitched on her shirt. I was amused. I thought the turtles were very fitting, and not only for the 'slow and less' train. How else to symbolize the progression my life was taking?

The conductor told us that the mechanical fault had been fixed and asked us to board the train. "Please proceed with care," she said.

We got back onto the train and settled comfortably into our compartment once more.

The girls played dominoes while their father read a book. Meanwhile, I was going through my notes and had questions. A lot of questions.

My friend looked up from his book; he could tell I was fidgety. "Ask me anything you want," he said.

"Well, for one, I'd like to understand how you arrived at being able to see the world through your heart and not solely through your eyes. It seems that you possess something special that few of us will ever have the privilege of acquiring. I also want to experience the world in this way."

"My friend," he said, "it's a long story."

"It's okay, we have plenty of time."

We laughed and the girls turned to us, wondering what the fuss was all about. My friend began to talk as I listened attentively.

"I can't recall the specific time or place I experienced what some refer to as a spiritual awakening. On this short but beautiful journey we call life, I, like you, bought into the system. Everything had to be a polished trophy: the job, the titles and the toys. I wanted more, much more. But as the years went by, I began to realize that more was never going to be enough. Something profound was missing. I felt an emotional void but knew it wouldn't be filled by a better job or more money. I think the universe picked up on this because, at some point, I began seeing, feeling and hearing things I wouldn't have noticed before. This happened when I started paying more attention to life. Simple experiences would leave lasting impressions. I began to hear birds singing outside my office. At first I thought this was unusual but, in truth, they had probably been performing for years but their music had fallen on deaf ears. I'm glad they didn't give up.

"Small things like that made me realize that something was changing in the way I was relating to and interacting with the world. I was beginning to feel and experience things with such awe, as a child does when it encounters snow for the first time. There were lots of spectacular moments; I called them 'mini-revelations.'

"Some of them happened in my own backyard. For instance, I used to consider gardening a burden. It wasn't something I particularly wanted to do but something I had to do. It felt like a chore. I wasn't aware of it, but as I labored in the garden, week after week, it began working on me in its own mysterious way. I wasn't able to grow an enviable garden but guess what happened? The garden grew on me. Season after season, the garden planted its seeds in me and waited patiently until one day I blossomed like the fragrant jasmine flowers I had planted the previous year. I came to recognize that my gardening experience resembled life. Tending a garden requires patience and offers no guarantees that the cherry tomatoes you plant today will provide for your salad tomorrow. Our participation in life works like that too. Our sweat, tears and sacrifices today can create openings to better things tomorrow. There are no guarantees but the possibilities of our efforts bearing fruit increase if we tend to the garden of our life.

"The realization that a burden may actually be a catalyst for something better completely transformed my life. Now, to answer your question, the first sign of a spiritual awakening, if that's what you want to call it, is when you begin to feel the rapture of life in the mundane moments and the activities you perform daily. These are common things you wouldn't have noticed before because you were too busy looking to the future or being trapped in the past. It could be noticing the sound of your breath when everything around is quiet. It could be sipping on a cup of coffee alone and, for no apparent reason, feeling overwhelmed with joy and gratitude. It could be seeing a line of trees from your bedroom and noticing their infinite glory for the first time. A serene feeling spreads inside as you begin to see and feel the sacredness in everything around you.

"Like signposts that help direct the traffic and keep it moving, the universe guides us with life posts. They're cues, each intended to nudge us in the direction of a spiritual awakening. They often appear as mysterious coincidences and we notice them with more frequency the more aware or present we become. The signs are everywhere but they're not so apparent or clear in the beginning.

"It's especially true when we're on the 'fast and more' train and it becomes clearer when we slow down and become more present. I remember a few such occasions. Once, I went out jogging and after a while I sat down on a wooden bench to catch my breath and recover. To my surprise, a butterfly with vivid colors landed on my knee. I was amused. It occurred to me that chasing happiness is a lot like chasing a butterfly. Not easy but if you stay still, happiness can come to you just like the butterfly did to me.

"Suddenly a cat jumped on my lap and scared the butterfly away. I reflected on how sitting still in one place had attracted two beautiful moments. I realized that the universe had begun rewarding me during the times when I slowed down and waited patiently. It seemed that doing nothing was actually doing something; it encouraged me to be present.

"Like butterflies and cats, answers arrive in moments of stillness, when you least expect them. As the cat continued snuggling on my lap, I saw a group of joggers run past us. And it hit me: patience is a form of conserving mental energy and the more I practiced it, the more I began to notice problems dissolving over time. I knew from personal experience that I could cover longer distances if I ran at a slower pace. Running fast meant burning precious fuel. Hurrying or rushing along was like burning emotional and physical energy. At some point, your energy dries up and when that happens you break down.

"On the other hand, conserving energy is like practicing patience. To go far in life, as in running, you sometimes have to slow down, ponder, pray or meditate. Whatever works for you."

***

"I can't explain what prompted me to visit a cemetery on my way back home from a stressful day at work. It's only minutes from my house and I've been driving by it ever since I was a child. The spirits were probably calling me to pay them a visit. I couldn't ignore them and I answered their call. As I entered the cemetery's main gateway, I felt this strange sensation.

"I heard a voice from out of nowhere. It whispered in my ear and said, 'Welcome home.'

"I brushed the imaginary voice aside and mumbled to myself that this definitely wasn't home. I told the spirits that I was simply visiting to pay my respects before going home to my family. There were hundreds of tombstones, perhaps thousands, in countless shapes and sizes, stretching in all directions. As I walked past the graves, one in particular stood out. It was well-kept and surrounded by flowers. A few feet away, there was another grave with no flowers, just weeds. I don't know if it was a coincidence but the better-kept grave had attracted two cats. They were lying on their sides.

"I continued walking and a few moments later, I saw a black cat sitting on top of a well-maintained tombstone. The cat gave me a suspicious look as I walked briskly by.

"I wondered if the presence of the cats had anything to do

with their feeling connected to the spirits of the people whose bodies were buried below. Were the cats attracted to the purity of their souls? What good deeds had they done, which years, if not decades, later would attract flowers in full bloom and curious black cats? And what crimes, if any, had those souls committed to attract weeds? Were the cats attracted to the flowers, the souls or both? Or maybe neither? Perhaps I was just entertaining the absurdity of random thoughts.

"I turned back on the same path I had taken earlier. It was getting dark but I didn't even make it halfway through the cemetery. I began paying closer attention to the tombstones. As I walked past each one, I took a mental note of each person's age and wondered about their cause of death. Some had died as babies while others made it into their nineties. With a few exceptions, the vast majority had died in their sixties and seventies. That's when it hit me that I had fewer days ahead of me than behind. We rationalize mortality but it only sinks in after every cell of our body becomes aware of how brief and fragile our existence on this planet is.

"Awareness definitely played a key role in my awakening. Recurring thoughts of mortality put life into perspective. They should be welcomed. I began to appreciate and feel gratitude for everything. I'd look at things and thank the universe, sometimes quietly and other times out loud. It wasn't uncommon for me to sit at the end of my bed and just stare out of the window in complete awe of the garden and city beyond. Sometimes I'd see migratory birds pass by, squawking as if to wish me good morning before heading off to their destination. I'd wave frantically to grab their attention and shout, 'Good morning to you too.'

"I'd see a lazy cat napping comfortably next to a smiling black dog and I'd know they were best friends. I'd walk on sandy beaches and allow the waves to roll up until they kissed my bare feet. Sometimes I'd leap over the crashing waves and other times I'd surrender to their salty kisses. I began feeling connected to life in a way that made the experiences around me richer and more precious. This didn't mean that my problems suddenly vanished, but I observed something incredible: the more grateful I was, the more everything around me looked brighter and just more beautiful.

"On another occasion I was attending a business seminar. There were about two hundred people seated in the auditorium and as I observed them, it occurred to me that, decades on, not one of the participants in the event would be alive. Of course, it's obvious but it didn't sink in or register at the time in a way that could have actually enhanced my life. At some point, every child, man and woman in every town, country and continent won't be around. I began to think of men and women who, decades ago, were my present age. I wondered if they were still alive and, if so, what physical and mental state they were in. Were they able to walk unassisted? Were they on medication? Were they happy or were they miserable?

"There were more life posts. One took place inside a hospital. I had gone in for a regular checkup and was handed a call number. As I sat patiently waiting for my turn, I observed the worry on everybody's face and I knew some would leave the hospital with a deeper appreciation of life. I was one of them. As I looked around, I saw decaying bodies, some neglected by their owners and a few about to depart. They weren't just ailing bodies but vivid reminders of how grateful we should be for the privilege to witness life."

I took notes. "Spend time visiting hospitals and cemeteries." I told my friend what I had written and he quickly added that, however useful that was, everybody has to embark on their own journey of personal growth and self-discovery. What led to his awakening didn't necessarily translate to someone else's awakening.

I was disappointed but I brightened when he added, "Whichever path you take, all roads intersect at the source. It's a divine moment on your journey. An awakening happens that impacts every cell of your body. It's sacred and blissful. It's a shift, a rebirth of who you were and who you've become. As I said earlier, anything can spark an inward journey. For some it can be a traumatic experience, like the sudden loss of a loved one, while for others it is merely a longing to make sense of their place in the world."

***

As I pondered on the things he had said, I wondered if I would ever come close to feeling the same way. I looked around and the answer hit me when I noticed a wooden sign above the entrance of our carriage. It read, "Slow and Less." My gosh, I thought, we really do see what we feel inside.

I smiled. Instinctively I knew I was heading inwards. I would wait patiently. I thanked my friend for opening up and sharing so much about himself. I didn't feel comfortable asking another question but I couldn't resist. "If you don't mind," I said hesitantly, "can you tell me what it means to be spiritually awakened and how your life is any different from those who aren't?"

He said, "For one thing, every moment I experience, including this one with you, feels like the universe is handing me a gift I don't deserve."

"Come on," I interrupted. "Don't you think you're exaggerating just a little bit?"

He laughed. "No, it's true. Really," he said. "It's like unwrapping a gift every second of the day."

"But how can that be?" I wondered aloud, but deep inside I knew it to be true.

"It's a wonderful feeling but it's hard to explain, my new friend continued. "Life keeps handing you gifts when you hold a deep sense of gratitude and appreciation for everything, including difficult moments. It's not easy but trust me, somehow the universe rewards you when it's no longer about you. The journey inward is a journey to connect with something far bigger than yourself. When the connection is made, say with the spirit, the light, consciousness or whatever you want to call it, miracles begin to happen. In my case, they arrive as presents and you're one of them."

"Wow," I said. That's very kind of you to say so. Thank you."

"It's not that complicated. If only people would realize they're surrounded by overwhelming beauty that doesn't cost a thing."

"I know I've heard that before and it's a cliché but, indeed, 'The best things in life are free.'"

"Do you know why? Because they're non-material and come from within. Those are priceless."

My notes were overflowing with invaluable content that I knew would serve me later in life.

"Back to your question," he said, "being spiritually awakened or conscious is the difference between living with light or living in complete darkness. It's a life with richer experiences and fewer imaginary burdens."

I asked if he could give an example of what it meant to live with light.

His eyes lit up. "It's astonishing what living with light means. Difficult people or traffic jams no longer become a source of stress and anxiety. You look around and say, 'I am here,' while they look around and say, 'Why am I here?' That's what living with light means."

***

I told him I could relate to most of the things he had said but I still had my doubts. I asked him what he thought of people who were skeptical towards others who appeared to live more consciously or in a more awakened state.

He replied, "It's not up to you to prove anything to anybody. When actions are fueled by love, people notice and their doubts diminish over time. There's no better proof than someone beaming with love. The point isn't to prove it but to live it. Actions derived from love leave a trail of evidence so clear that, over time, even the skeptics become converts. There will always be doubters and people suspicious of your motives. They'll point fingers and accuse you of being delusional. Don't let their opinions bother you. If they insist on proof, try asking them if they can use science to prove you wrong or whether or not they believe, as you do, that things exist which the eyes can't see or detect even under the most powerful microscopes.

"You'll see. They'll have a hard time proving you wrong while admitting that things exist which they can't see. We know that thoughts, memories and emotions exist but we can't objectively prove that they do. There are so many things that exist that can't be quantified by science or understood by our mind. Reason can only take us so far and that's why for anything beyond that, we should take a leap of faith. Encourage doubters, at their own pace and in their own way, to travel inwardly beyond reason. They might be hesitant but some will eventually arrive at a point in their lives when they're ready. You'll recognize who they are because you were one of them. Their joy is no longer derived from outward pleasures but, instead, from inward ones that emanate from the heart like love, compassion and gratitude."

Nine

The Golden Couple

The door of our compartment slid wide open and a couple holding hands entered.

"Mind if we join?" asked the gentleman.

"Not at all, there's plenty of room," said my friend.

They appeared to be in their seventies. The man was about five foot eleven, bald and looked to be in good shape. His wife had piercing blue eyes and long silver hair that graced her shoulders. They sat right next to me.

The lady turned to me and said, "Silver hair. Golden couple."

"Excuse me?" I said.

"We're celebrating our 50th wedding anniversary."

Everybody in the carriage started laughing, including my friend's daughters. I knew this was going to be a fun trip with so much to learn from the golden couple who had been married for fifty years.

"I see you still use a pen and pad," she said.

"Yeah, I enjoy writing," I replied.

"Great," she said, "I love talking."

Her husband jumped in and said, "Honey, can you please be a little quieter. We've only just met them. Maybe they want some peace and quiet."

"No, it's okay," said my friend, "please continue. We could use a good laugh and learn more about the secrets of a lasting marriage. Girls, are you listening? This advice could come in handy a few years from now when you start dating!"

We all burst into laughter.

The woman was hilarious and I told her so.

"First of all, you've got to have a sense of humor, not just in your relationship but with life too. Be silly. Don't take everything so seriously or personally."

She turned to me and said, "Taking notes?"

I was.

"Boys and girls, it's simple. There are tons of books on relationships but it's not that complicated. Of course, what worked for us might not work for everybody. For starters, I always have the last word, right love?" she said, glancing mischievously at her husband.

He nodded and said, "That's right, honey."

We all laughed again.

She continued, "Joking aside, we've had our ups and downs. It is not always smooth sailing but we've never gone to sleep with a grudge against each other. We don't keep score because nobody wins with more points in a relationship. There are times when residue remains after an argument and, yes, there are many, but like a magician with a magic wand, a good night's sleep can make disputes disappear the next morning.

"And if they don't dissipate the next morning, they vanish

the morning after that. Who would have guessed that sleeping isn't just good for your health and marriage but for problem-solving too? How many times have you gone to sleep with a problem, only to wake up with the answer the next day? I find that incredible, don't you? Closing our eyes with a problem and then waking up the next morning with a solution. Now that's what I call magic."

She asked how my notes were coming along and I shared the following: "Relationships require patience and, if you don't have patience, try sleeping on whatever's bothering you. It works like magic."

"Excellent," she said, "I couldn't have expressed it better myself!"

"Is that it?" I asked.

"Well, in a way, yes, but it's essential to forgive, let go and not dwell on the past."

"Definitely," added her husband.

"If you think about it," continued the lady, "these are some of the essential ingredients that make up love. They're qualities we all possess but seldom express. Imagine if we did so on a regular basis? My gosh, I think most therapists would go out of business," she said with a smile.

"Something else: You're going to disagree on a lot of things but that's not the problem. The problem is losing your temper and saying things you don't really mean and wish you could take back. That's why we have to choose our words carefully. Spiteful ones are like carrying heavy bricks in a backpack; if you don't set them aside, they end up accumulating until they become too much to bear."

"I like how you're framing this," added her husband.

"The heart, like your backpack," she continued, "can only hold so much before it breaks. That's why trying to work things out is more important than proving a point. It takes some sacrificing but it's the right thing to do if you want to get along with your partner. Think about it. Aren't arguments just futile disagreements between egos posturing for control? I'll explain what I mean. Have you ever borrowed money and had to pay it back with interest?"

I nodded.

"Well, unresolved arguments are just like having to pay interest. There's an emotional cost to be had for this argument and the longer you wait to resolve it the higher it becomes. It's just like accrued interest on a loan."

I asked if she could elaborate.

"Well," she said, "every action has a consequence. Some are good and some are bad. The not-so-good ones come back to haunt you. Let's take running a business and ruining your health as an example. Unresolved business problems can lead to financial ruin just as neglecting your health over time can result in you dying prematurely. It takes a lot of maturity and awareness to figure this out and not all couples do. At some point in your relationship and your life in general, you have to understand that some of your opinions just aren't worth defending at the expense of jeopardizing your health or relationship. And trust me, applying this will do wonders for your sanity."

"But how can I do that?" I asked.

She said, "Start by telling yourself 'It doesn't matter.' These three words can change your life."

Her husband pointed at his bald head as if to jokingly imply his wife had something to do with it.

We both smiled.

She continued, "You think that what you're arguing about is the difference between day and night but once you step back and see things more objectively, you end up realizing it's no big deal. I believe the same is true for a lot of things in life. In fact, I can't remember what most of our arguments were about. Can you honey?" she asked her husband.

He shook his head.

"Who knows?" she wondered aloud. "Maybe it's because we're getting older or because we're just getting wiser."

"Definitely wiser," added her husband, who seemed proud of hearing what his wife had to say on the topic of relationships.

She went on. "Obviously, a lot of things matter so let me be clear about what I mean. Let's say you go out with two friends. It's getting late and you're feeling hungry. One of your friends recommends a popular Chinese restaurant but you insist on dining out at another place. Sure enough, tensions rise so you turn to your third friend and ask her where she'd like to eat. Her reply: 'It doesn't matter as long as I'm with you.' She's okay with eating at the Chinese or any other place. But wait. You end up going to the Chinese restaurant and now have to decide between sitting indoors or outdoors. Again, your friend says she doesn't mind as long as she's with the both of you. She's easygoing. She's happy either way. I bet her evening's going to turn out a lot better than yours, don't you? So choose your preferences carefully because the fewer you have, the better life gets.

"Think how pleasant life can be when you're open to going anywhere, under any weather conditions, as long as you're around the people you love."

Her wise husband added, "As long as you're around good people, it doesn't matter where you are, because people become

44

the place and the place becomes the makeup of those people."

I was blown away. I repeated, "It doesn't matter" in my mind and got goosebumps. I knew the significance of those words because I had heard them uttered to me many times before but this time they sank in. I knew that being flexible or going with the flow would be life-changing. There would be more win-wins.

The husband went on to share some marriage tips of his own.

"I'm no expert but I'll tell you some of the things that have worked for us. Be quick to admit your mistakes. It's not always easy but telling your partner how sorry you were or admitting they had a good point goes a long way to setting things right. I've also found holding back to be just as good for our relationship. Sure, some things are worth reacting to but not everything. Feeling upset, outraged or angry over something is part of being human but blasting out is like adding fuel to the fire. Tensions in a relationship are just like fires, they dissolve when denied fuel.

"Just keep in mind that some things are worth brushing aside."

"Oh, now I see. In one ear, out the other," joked his wife.

"No, that's not what I meant. It's in line with what you said earlier about it not mattering. On the contrary, listening to your partner is just as important in a relationship as flour is to baking bread; it's one of the key ingredients. The problem is we don't know how to listen. Talk less and listen more. It's not a competition. You don't have to react to every comment your partner makes. Instead, consider each argument as an exercise in self-control. You'll be impressed to see how it helps you to become a better person. It teaches you to be more patient and understanding and to value the true meaning of love. It depends, of course, on the circumstances of each relationship but, more often than not, unconditional love wins out every time.

"Another key point, and it's probably the most difficult one, is learning to silence your ego in order to make room for love to flourish. If you can do that, I can assure you that any relationship will blossom. There'll be fewer escalations, tension and tears. And how's that for advice from someone who's celebrating his 50th wedding anniversary today?"

I smiled.

***

"Tell me about yourself," asked the golden anniversary man I had come to admire.

I rolled my eyes and paused for what seemed like eternity. There was complete silence in the compartment as everybody waited for me to introduce myself.

"Not long ago," I said, "I felt I was traveling on a train called 'fast and more,' with a way of life that left little time for self-reflection. I remember how friends and family would gather around my birthday cake and sing 'Happy Birthday'. As they sang, I'd just stare at the candles and wonder how it was possible for a decade to pass by as if it were a day. The obvious was beginning to sink in: that time was finite and I wanted to make the most of what was left. I wanted to squeeze more out of life. I had accomplished a lot by society's metrics but I still felt that something was missing. I had wondered for years where and what that something was until I serendipitously came across it, right inside here."

I tapped the left side of my chest twice with my right hand. "It didn't happen overnight but that's when I decided to change course and pursue a life that wasn't so fast. Along the way, I

46

began taking notes on the transition from outward pleasures and possessions to inner ones."

"You should share those insights with the world by writing a book," said my friend.

I thanked him but said that such a task would be more difficult than climbing the highest mountain in the world. I didn't think I was qualified to write anything that people would find worthy of reading.

"That's crazy," he said with a stern voice. "It doesn't matter what people think. What matters is the joy you get from writing, from expressing yourself in the way that singers, painters and dancers do. For a moment, forget about the book. Just relax and enjoy the creative process of getting there, even if you never arrive."

I was confused.

"Listen, you love keeping a diary, don't you?"

I nodded with absolute certainty.

"Well, consider a book the final destination while the real joy lies in the act of writing, in other words, in the journey. It's the result of you placing one word next to another until you fill a page and eventually enough pages to complete a chapter. End up with a few solid chapters and you've got yourself a book."

He was right. Something clicked. I realized how hard it can be to appreciate the present moment when all our attention is focused on some future goal, like publishing a book. It became clear why writing was so much fun. It forced me to be present and enjoy every moment, just as so many wise people have pointed out. I relished that idea and wrote, "The journey IS the destination. Be present and keep writing."

***

"We have three children and two grandchildren," said our proud friend.

His wife jumped in and said, "Honey, you told me you would be quiet, but you're doing all the talking."

He smiled and knew she was joking. I liked how they teased each other.

He continued, "I'm a few weeks shy of my eightieth birthday but if I were to write a book it'd be partly about bees."

My friend and I looked at each other and wondered what he meant.

"Really? We'd love to hear more about it," I said with a bit of trepidation.

"Me too," said his wife as she winked back at him.

"Well," he said, "I'd write about living with gratitude and love."

We listened intently.

He began by asking the girls if they were afraid of bees. The older one nodded and said, "Just a little."

"Years ago, before you and even your parents were born, my father had a dream to become a beekeeper. It'd be his first job out of high school. He was a young man, around eighteen years old, and he needed to borrow money from the bank in order to purchase some beehives. The manager was a little skeptical and not convinced that my father would be able to earn enough money to pay back the loan. He asked what he had in the form of collateral and my dad enthusiastically replied he had a stack of books and a bicycle. He was confident that this would be enough to convince the banker to grant him a loan. The bank manager wasn't impressed but my father, wise beyond his years, removed any doubts the banker had when he said, "Sir, honey makes money. Where else can you find a job that has a thousand employees working for you day and night without pay?"

"Of course, he was referring to the honeybees. The banker was impressed with his response and approved the loan that would go on to finance my father's beekeeping business.

"Girls, it's true, bees can sting but they're also essential to life. Did you know that, if they ever became extinct, the world would experience massive food shortages?"

The girls' eyes lit up in astonishment.

"Including ice cream and chocolate?" asked the younger one.

"Yes, including ice cream and chocolate because they're both made from milk. Most cows feed on plants that are pollinated by bees."

"Pollinated?" asked the little one.

"Pollination is like the kiss of life for the plant world."

The girls giggled.

"Without one, you can't have the other."

My friend and I listened in admiration.

"I was alone in the wilderness one day. Wildflowers blanketed the landscape and bees were buzzing in every direction. I turned my head and spotted one trapped in a puddle of water. It was swirling around in circles and fighting for survival. It tried hard to fly away but couldn't because its wings were wet and hopelessly bound to the water. I knew that if I didn't do anything it was going to die, so I placed my index finger right next to the bee. I held my breath and watched the bee struggle onto my finger. It slowly made its way to the tip of my finger where it stopped to recover while I pointed it towards the blazing sun.

"I wondered if it was going to sting me or spare me the agony for having saved it. I wasn't worried. Time stood still as I watched the bee attempt to escape its fate and fly back to freedom. It flapped its wet wings and with help from the sun it flew to salvation. I turned to the heavens and shed a tear of gratitude for having witnessed such a special moment."

The girls clapped their hands on hearing that the bee had flown to freedom and the little one said, "You're our hero. You saved our planet and all the children who love ice cream and chocolate!"

Her dad added, "Adults too, let's order some."

I asked my golden friend if the lesson of the bee was one of gratitude.

"The lesson," he said, "is that magic moments like the one I experienced with the bee exist everywhere. They exist in the mundane day-to-day activities we perform unconsciously, like going to work, washing the dishes or taking a shower. Those are moments to be grateful for, not for wishing we were somewhere else. I'm not saying we should stop dreaming of traveling and doing other things but we should definitely start by being grateful for what we have instead of dwelling on what we don't have. If being grateful becomes a part of who you are and how you interact with life, you end up richer than all the kings and queens who ever ruled the world."

"Why?" I asked curiously.

"Because conquerors want 'more' and 'more' is never enough. It's elusive, an insatiable appetite that even wealth and power can't fill."

I reflected on my life and thought that, in some way I had once been a king and perhaps still was in many ways. But I felt that this was beginning to change. I was becoming more grateful for things I wouldn't have noticed before, like the good company I was in, the conversations I had and even a simple cup of coffee. I recognized they all began with the letter C and told my travel companions we should call them the three C's of happiness; the simple things we can be grateful for: conversations, company and coffee.

"That's a great idea," said the golden man as he was being served a scoop of ice cream and a slice of chocolate cake.

"Daddy, daddy!" yelled the little one as she pointed to the chocolate cake. "Four C's of gratitude, with chocolate cake!"

"Excellent point!" said her proud father, with a wide smile across his face.

I wrote, "The four C's of happiness include good company, conversation, coffee and chocolate."

***

I thanked him for sharing his story about gratitude.

"This chocolate cake is delicious," said his wife. "I want to thank the people who made it, the lady who served it and, of course, my lovely husband who paid for it. Honey, I think our friends are anxious to hear another of your stories."

And so her husband began:

"Gentlemen, when I was your age, my father was about ninety years old. He was a gifted storyteller. Some of his stories were so outlandish it was hard to distinguish between fact and fiction. He could draw an audience and hold their attention from beginning to the end. I often wondered if the stories he told were true or not but I figured, hey, why let the truth get in the way of a great story?

"He also loved telling jokes. There was one about experiencing orgasms in nature. I felt embarrassed and terribly uncomfortable in the presence of guests I didn't know and I apologise for using the word in front of your daughters," he said to our friend. "It wasn't until years later I understood what he meant. He wasn't joking and it wasn't fiction. Let me explain.

"One bright sunny morning, I set off to go trekking. Along the way I walked past a grove of lemon trees and jasmine flowers. The air was bursting with aromas. I thought how amazing it would be if I could replicate the fragrance and bottle the scent. I was running out of water and about to take a break when I heard some dogs barking in the foreground. I wasn't scared and I wanted to approach them. That's when I saw a group of men and women picking olives. The dogs continued to bark until their owner commanded them to be quiet.

"I said, 'It's okay, I love animals.'

"'Great,' he said, 'anyone who loves animals and particularly my dogs is welcome on my property like family. You must love life and music too.'

"'Very much so,' I replied.

"'Good, then join us for some red wine, bread and olives. Wine's the preferred drink of the gods and we've got to honor them.'

"I accepted the invitation, despite knowing that hiking and wine made for a hazardous combination. The man had dark wavy hair and a beard the length of his neck. He firmly gripped what appeared to be a wooden pole or walking stick. He looked like a rock star but could have easily been mistaken for a shepherd if he had a flock of sheep around.

"He asked me what kind of music I liked, and I told him anything that included a guitar and a strong vocalist.

'Really?' he asked with a huge smile on his face. 'You won't believe it, but I've travelled the world as a professional musician playing guitar.'

"My hunch was right. I knew I recognized him from somewhere. He looked familiar but I didn't know which group he performed with. He poured a second glass of wine and asked me where I was going. I pointed to the mountain peak in the north.

"'Be careful,' he said, 'mysterious things happen up there.'

"I wondered what he meant by 'mysterious things' but I didn't ask, probably out of fear of knowing. It was strange but I felt relaxed in the company of this celebrity I didn't recognize.

"He began talking about music, energy, people and vibrations. 'I'm a music guy. I've been playing the guitar for over thirty years in concerts around the world, from small towns like Ames, Iowa to crazy cities like Los Angeles and London.'

"'That's incredible," I said with admiration. 'And what did you learn about people or yourself on this journey?'

"'Great question, brother. Love your energy. I think of every person, including you, as a musical instrument. We perform in concerts every day.'

"I didn't get it.

"'Let me explain. For decades, I was trying to see how I could connect my passion for music to a better understanding of the human condition. It became clear to me that we're all musical instruments, unique and beautiful in our own way. Musical instruments, like people, vibrate at certain frequencies. Think of it this way. Imagine the words people say as musical notes. They're either in tune or out of sync. Tuned instruments, usually good people, have the potential to transform how you feel. It's incredible what happens when you surround yourself with like-minded energy. It's like being in a concert and listening to your favorite songs. Are you with me?'

"I nodded and asked if he could elaborate.

"'Well,' he said, 'people vibrate at various frequencies, mostly shaped by their experiences and their personal beliefs. Combined, they forge a musical instrument that vibrates at a particular note or frequency. Similar vibrations are attracted to each other as we are now. Can you feel it? It's as if we've known each other forever?'

"I nodded in agreement.

"'When I perform at shows, I get to experience what it's like when thousands of fans simultaneously connect to my music and unite as one. It's surreal. Imagine the sight, the bond created when a sea of people vibrates at the same frequency, all meeting at a level far beyond the color of their skin, gender, judgment and even beliefs. It's divine, just like wine.'

"I smiled. It was time for me to get going but I opted to stay a little more. We drank, laughed, danced and sang.

"'A little tipsy!' he exclaimed, 'Feel the energy?'

"Of course I did.

"He gave me a firm hug and wished me well on my long walk to the top of the mountain.

"As I left, the man's wife brought me a bag of ripe pomegranates and sweet dates. She said, 'You'll need the extra energy. It's going to fuel your climb to the top of the mountain which should take about two hours from here.'

"I filled the empty bottle with water and thanked them for their hospitality."

My golden friend's chance encounter – or not – with a rock star in an open field provided a goldmine of life lessons.

His wife said, "His trekking adventure happened for real and I could hardly believe it when he told me about it. It altered the way he saw the world."

My notebook was beginning to run out of space. Three blank pages were left. I wrote: "People are like musical instruments and the ones that are fine-tuned seem to be rewarded. Reminder to self: See notes on karma."

My friend continued his story about his journey to the peak of the mountain.

"I walked for an hour and began feeling dizzy. I wasn't sure if it was because of the wine I had drunk earlier or exhaustion from having walked in high temperatures all morning. It was almost noon and I figured it would take another hour before I reached the summit. I wanted to take a break and found temporary relief under a pine tree. I lay flat on my back in the small patch of shade and spread my arms and legs wide open like children do when forming snow angels.

"My mind drifted aimlessly when suddenly a pine cone the size of a tennis ball dropped an arm's length from my head. I heard a cracking sound as soon as it landed. I stared at it for what seemed like eternity and observed every detail as if it was the most beautiful thing I had ever set eyes on.

"I felt something strange but beautiful, an inner peace, a kind of kinship not just with the pine cone but also with everything around me. Trees were greener, scents were stronger and birds were singing as if to greet me. I got back on my feet and pulled some dates and pomegranates out of my backpack. Later, I felt immortal on top of the mountain."

***

His story about connecting with a pine cone reminded me of his father's experience with the honeybee. Both mentioned feeling calm and peaceful, something I could relate to. Nature, especially when you're alone in the wilderness, has that effect on people.

He continued, "Gentlemen, are you still interested in the part about orgasms?"

"Yes honey, they are," said his wife. She kissed him on his left cheek and asked the father if she could take his daughters for a walk around the train. She had heard about a games room and thought it would be an opportunity to stretch and have some fun with the girls.

"Sure," said my friend.

The girls were delighted. He wished them well and said, "Love you, girls. Be sure to behave yourselves and have a great time with the lady."

The girls giggled but I wondered how they felt about not having their mother around to kiss them. As they went holding each other's hands. I was moved by the wisdom of the lady to remove the girls before the orgasms story and by the evident love between the two daughters and their father.

As the sliding door shut behind them, her husband turned to my friend and said, "Your girls are so well-behaved, and I sense the spirit of their mother in both of them."

My friend gently bowed his head and placed his hand over his chest. He thanked him for his kind words and asked how he knew about his wife.

"I don't know anything about your wife, but I could feel her presence in this cabin and she shines brightly through your children. You don't have to see things to believe they exist."

I knew exactly what he was talking about. I also sensed his wife's presence and spirit emanating through his daughters. The compartment fell silent as we looked out of the window and saw a flock of doves flying gracefully over a long stretch of virgin land.

Our golden friend said, "I can't believe what I'm seeing."

"What do you mean?" I asked.

"The doves, the doves," exclaimed our storyteller.

"They played a significant role in my spiritual awakening. I didn't finish my story about what happened at the top of the mountain. Do you remember when the rock star said mysterious things happen there? Well he was right."

"Is this the part about orgasms?" asked my bold friend.

"Yes, it is but it's not what you think. I eventually made it to the summit. I was exhausted and wondered if I'd make it back home in time before the sun set. The view was spectacular. If you were a painter from the vantage point I had, you'd produce a masterpiece. From the mountaintop you could see the earth touch the ocean, the ocean touch the sky and the sky touch eternity. It was a breathtaking sight, recorded for life in my memory. I felt an overwhelming sense of joy and serenity. Then something strange happened. A white dove landed not far from where I sat. I began to cry. I thought I was hallucinating and had to pinch myself to make sure I wasn't imagining things. First it was a pine cone that landed next to me and now a friendly white dove. Did the dove, a symbol of purity, peace and love, arrive with a message and, if so, what was it? I thought deeply about it until it became crystal clear. I wiped the tears from my watery eyes and understood what my father had meant by 'orgasms in nature'. He was describing moments like the one I felt with the pine cone and dove. It can happen to anyone, anywhere and when you least expect it."

The girls returned from the game room, hiding something behind their backs.

"Daddy, we had so much fun just like we used to play with mommy."

"The girls have a surprise for you," said the wise woman.

"I love surprises," said their father.

The youngest one revealed a drawing of a dove and handed it to her father. The drawing included lots of red hearts and the words "I love you."

The father hugged his daughter and said, "I love you too. You're just as talented as your mother was and I'm sure she was guiding you with every stroke of your hand."

"She definitely was," said his daughter feeling proud and glowing with satisfaction.

"That's amazing. Your husband was just telling us about his meeting with the dove on the summit."

Then my friend's elder daughter handed me a drawing of a dozen pine cones scattered around an evergreen tree. It was hard to believe that a child could sketch something so beautiful. The significance of the pine cone and the moment wasn't lost on me. I understood what it meant to my new friend who asked his wife, in a playful way if he'd get a drawing too.

"Of course, dear," she said as she handed him a colorful painting that caused his jaw to drop. "Happy anniversary," she said.

He held it up so we could all see the painting. We clapped our hands.

He turned to his wife and said, "Honey, this is a masterpiece."

She had painted the spectacular view that her husband had seen from the summit many years ago. It was just as he had described it. At the bottom of the page you could see delicate paint strokes of sun-dried land in various tints of yellow and brown. Directly above the land, she had used her paintbrush to apply dark shades of blue across the page. It perfectly depicted the ocean. Above the ocean, in lighter blue strokes, she had painted a breathtaking sky that included lean clouds, some shaped in letters. The clouds seemed to contain a subliminal message but I wasn't quite sure what it was. Finally, above the tranquil blue sky, were thin strips of yellow that slowly faded to the top of the page, becoming lighter and lighter until the last few strokes were as white as the paper it was painted on. My mind went to the wise man's words when he had said, "The earth touched the ocean, the ocean touched the sky and the sky touched eternity."

The train came to a stop. The father and his daughters had reached their destination. We exchanged pleasantries and promised to keep in touch. Once again, I thanked my friend's daughters for the beautiful pine cone sketch and told them how special they were. They blushed. I knew exactly what I was going to do with the sketch. I was going to use it as a bookmark and as a reminder to be grateful for everything, even the things that others find insignificant. I told her I'd include her sketch in my book if I ever wrote one. They embraced the golden couple, said goodbye and stepped off the train as new passengers boarded. Moments later the train began to move again.

I couldn't stop wondering how both girls shared their mother's vision and whether she was watching in admiration. I wanted to include those thoughts on my notepad but every page was full. It was time to replace it with a new one I had in my backpack. It was a gift I had received from a friend. She was known in the art world but preferred to live a secluded and rather anonymous life. I cherished the notepad because it blended her two talents as an artist and as a magician. The cover of the notepad depicted an eye that peered right back at you and would transform into a sun if you stared at it for about thirty seconds. I looked at the inside of the cover and read my friend's handwritten dedication: "To my dearest friend and soulmate, I hope you start seeing the world with your heart as wide open as the loving eye on the cover of this notepad."

I wasn't sure what she meant at the time but her signed message was perfectly clear today. I wondered if this could be an omen and turned to the golden couple for clarification. I held the cover up and asked them not to blink. They held each other's hands tightly just as excited kids about to play a new game.

"Honey, honey, do you see what I see?"

"Unbelievable," he said, "The eye becomes a sun."

I could tell he was overcome with emotion, not because of the optical illusion but because of the meaning behind it all.

He said, "Eyes and the sun are symbols of light and awakened states, the same elements that were present during my life-altering transformation on the summit."

I asked him to elaborate while I wrote with a burst of enthusiasm on my magical notepad.

"Personal transformations happen when there's a shift in awareness and perception. It can take years before it reveals itself or it can happen from one moment to the next. I'll use an analogy to explain an awakening. Take water, for example. Its boiling point is 100 degrees Celsius and the time it takes to reach that temperature depends on the amount of heat and pressure applied. Imagine heat and pressure as symbols of your life experiences. So let's say a divorce counts as eight degrees, being laid off counts as five degrees, and a life-threatening disease counts as twenty degrees. People have awakening points that can only be attained if their life experiences bring them closer to their personal boiling point. Of course, each person's boiling point varies based on their beliefs and life circumstances. A lot of people never come close to an awakened state but those who do are blessed for life."

"That's an interesting way of seeing it," I said. He added, "Awakenings surface over time but most are triggered by painful and often stressful events like a break-up, disease and death of a loved one. The solution is to surrender to whatever happened in the past, to somehow let it go. People think doing so is a weakness. It's not. It simply creates an environment, a healthy space for inner peace to settle in.

"It can take years or even decades before one arrives, if at all, to an understanding this. You see, something special happens when people become capable of transcending the unthinkable and even the unforgivable. They start seeing things as if they've acquired some type of new and supernatural sense."

I knew exactly what he was talking about and was eager to hear the rest of his story.

He continued, "We've heard of people who go through near-death experiences and afterwards admit to being happier than ever before. In a way, it's what sages have been professing for centuries: to die before we die, in order to appreciate our lives more fully today. We know that death can come knocking on our door when we least expect it, disguised as a phone call from our doctor with news about our health or as a red light that someone accidentally drove through on their way back home from work. Those who come close to death, who get a second chance, often end up engaging with life on a much deeper level than before."

I nodded, acknowledging that what he said wasn't so uncommon.

His wife added, "The closer we are to death, the closer we are to life."

I'm not sure I understood what she meant but thought it was significant and underlined it in my notes so I could ask about it later. I knew I didn't want to come close to dying and wondered if I had to cozy up with death in order to experience this elusive awakening they were talking about. All kinds of thoughts ran through my head. I knew it wasn't a goal to strive for but perhaps a deep longing we all had, a spiritual need that yearns to express itself. I thought of all the people I knew and realized that we were all on our own separate paths in the hope of experiencing something more meaningful, even as life-transforming as a spiritual awakening. I was convinced it can happen. It does sometimes.

"Now it's our turn to play a game with you," said his wife. "We enjoyed your notepad's optical illusion but I'd like to ask you to look into my eyes and tell me what you see."

I couldn't believe it; she was posing the same question as the elegant lady I had met at the station a while back. I happily obliged and said I saw a kind and gentle heart made of gold.

Her husband laughed, "Good one about the golden heart, especially on our fiftieth wedding anniversary."

"Speaking of hearts," she added, "hearts filled entirely with love experience the divine in every moment and in every human being. They begin to see a piece of themselves in everything."

My eyes lit up. There was something profound about what she had just said.

She continued, "Awakened spirits acquire an unspoken but universal language that allows them to connect with everything in life."

That sounded like a super power I wanted to acquire.

"Have you ever come across people moving their lips and gesturing as if chatting with someone but when you look around you don't see anyone? We walk past them every day. We think they're crazy but they're not."

I nodded. I knew exactly what she meant because I was also guilty of thinking they were lost souls. I'm sure that some suffered from some type of mental illness but a good number had acquired a sixth sense, the ability to connect with the metaphysical. I remember one lady in particular. She was about seventy years old. It seemed that, every day of the week, she was perfectly content sitting alone on a bench and marveling at everything around her for hours. She'd gaze endlessly towards the horizon and often talked to the trees. I frequently caught her blowing kisses to butterflies, mumbling something to the sky and greeting dogs that walked by. I thought she appeared lost and confused but I was mistaken. She didn't want anything more than the pleasure of that moment. She wasn't distracted by the people who'd walk by and think she was crazy, as I and so many others had done. She made me realize that life rewards us in moments of complete stillness, when time ceases to exist and love seems to flourish everywhere, as it did for her in the park.

I was beginning to enjoy and learn so much about myself on this journey and attributed it to becoming more aware of things I wouldn't have noticed if I hadn't slowed down. I felt my heart beginning to open up and see things that even my eyes couldn't see. I was beginning to like this new journey, and – dare I say it – the shift it was creating.

***

I dozed off and apologized to the golden couple after waking up.

"It's okay," said the woman. "Sleep is one of the natural states of the universe. Sooner or later, you and I are going to go to sleep and not wake up in the same form. And guess what? Flowers and bees will blossom because of that."

I knew she was talking about death and she confirmed this but, instead of using the word "dying," she referred to it as "passing on," or "transitioning from one state to another."

I asked her what she meant by flowers and bees thanking us for not waking up again.

She smiled, "Ah, it's one of the most beautiful things in the world. I believe we're living compost, here to serve humanity today and gardens tomorrow. Everybody's entitled to their own opinion about what happens but that's what I believe."

I was intrigued by her perspective but not convinced that it was, as she had described it, one of the most beautiful things in the world. She admitted to not having all the answers but it didn't matter. Compost was simply a metaphor for continuity and for her that was comforting.

Who was I to argue with her view of death? And surely, if it's not compost, I'd like to think it may be some type of energy, perhaps on a metaphysical level or channeled through other people. After all, I thought, aren't we genetically linked to our parents and ancestors? In a way, a bit of them is in us and a bit of us is in our children. What she said was enough to inspire me to write, "We're living compost to serve humanity today and gardens tomorrow."

Her husband was now fast asleep and since she enjoyed talking about mortality, I thought I'd ask her some more questions on the topic. "Are you afraid of dying?" I asked.

"Absolutely not," she said. "If you believe in the mighty intelligence of the universe, you've got to believe this isn't the end. Let me explain. Imagine you're a heap of sugar. What happens when you add a spoonful of sugar to a cup of hot tea or coffee?"

"It dissolves," I said.

"Exactly," she said, "you said 'dissolves' and not 'dies'. It changes form, from a physical state to a liquid state. It's still there but in a different form. And guess what, your drink is sweeter."

It was a different perspective on death but one I was beginning to like and even accept. Mention of coffee put us in the mood for ordering some. I spotted a service attendant who happened to walk by our carriage and I asked if we could place an order. He took it and, ten minutes later, our hot drinks arrived with a side plate of chocolate-filled croissants. I looked up at my friend and she winked right back at me.

"Try it," she said.

I knew what she meant. It's as if the clock had turned back forty years and I was a child again. I added sugar to my cup of coffee, stirred it and observed how the white crystals dissolved until they became invisible. Coffee would never be the same after this new way of looking at life and life beyond life.

"You see," she said, "just because you can't see the sugar, it doesn't mean it's not there. The same is true with life, we merge almost seamlessly to become one with the intelligent universe. We change forms and when we do, plants and bees thank us for becoming their compost. That's what I believe. I might be wrong, but no one came up with a convincing argument to prove me otherwise. Can you?" she asked with a smile.

I confessed I couldn't and encouraged her to keep talking.

"Listen," she said, "reason can only take us so far and anything beyond that requires a leap of faith. There's must be a bigger

65

story than the one we comprehend on earth. It's a story ingrained in all of humanity, that is this feeling of continuity or connecting with something bigger than ourselves. It's a story that our souls or spirits are dying to tell and, if we don't, we suffer in silence. Connecting with eternity is a universal yearning."

I couldn't quite grasp it all, but she said it with such enthusiasm and energy that I was convinced. Indeed, my thinking had evolved over the years. I remember first needing proof or empirical evidence before I could believe in anything. That was not the case anymore. After all, I couldn't see the white sugar crystals in my coffee but it tasted just the way I liked it.

Ten

The Briefcase

A handsome young man entered our carriage. Tall, clean-cut and carrying a leather briefcase, he had dark brown eyes and was probably in his mid-thirties. He looked like someone I could have related to many years before. He wore a conservative gray jacket with matching slim pants, a button up shirt with a collar to support his dark blue necktie. It was the classic business attire worn by millions of workers on the go, those on the 'fast and more' track. His uniform and smart briefcase reminded me of the way I used to commute to work.

"Hey, mind if I join you?" asked the young man.

"Of course not, you can sit right next to me," said my fun-hearted lady friend. "You're going home, aren't you?" she asked.

"Yeah, how did you know?" asked the businessman.

"'Cause you look tired," she said.

He nodded and said, "Very."

I welcomed the man and reassured him that everything would

be all right.

"Honey, wake up," said the lady to her husband. "I want to introduce you to our new guest."

He opened his eyes and said, "Hi there Mr. busy man, I mean businessman! Welcome to the wisest compartment on the entire train."

They shook hands and her husband teasingly said, "Hope you don't mind my chatty wife?"

"Honey, don't scare this handsome man away," laughed his wife.

"No worries, I'm here to learn and listen," he said.

I mentioned they were celebrating their fiftieth wedding anniversary.

The businessman said he couldn't believe his luck and added, "I can learn a lot about relationships from a golden couple because I'm going through a divorce and can't afford therapy."

Suddenly my golden friend jumped to his feet and shouted, "Just had a breakthrough."

"Another one!" remarked his wife.

He pointed to the businessman's briefcase and said, "I just realized something remarkable about life. This briefcase serves as a metaphor for understanding, in a way, the circle of life."

He seemed convinced that what he was about to reveal would answer most of our questions about life. All eyes and ears were fixed on him.

His wife asked him to sit down but he shook his head and preferred to remain upright.

Like a professor speaking to his students, he began by saying, "Imagine our life as a journey along an uneven road, consisting of random potholes, dead ends, steep hills, and fast descents. You get it, right?"

We nodded.

"A good part of our life is spent chasing things that we think will make us happy and successful. It could be striving for a promotion, wanting to buy a faster car or a bigger home. It could be wanting status, recognition or aiming for a certain position. The problem is, they'll never satisfy our insatiable appetite for 'more.' The better-paying job still gives you less than what your colleague earns, the fast car is overtaken by your friend's faster car, and the bigger home is smaller than your next-door neighbor's house."

He picked up the businessman's briefcase and said, "Most of our life, we're under the illusion that two steps forward and one step back is progress. As long as we inch closer to our goals, we think we'll eventually arrive at a place called utopia and live happily ever after. We're loyal to the briefcase, just like this one, a symbol of our ticket to a better life. But it's not sustainable. It comes at a price and it's usually in the form of unhappiness, deteriorating health and relationships."

He peered into my eyes and said, "I'm sure you can relate to the briefcase and acknowledge that we were once on the 'fast and more' train, can't you?" he asked.

I nodded and listened attentively to how this story would unfold.

He continued, "This isn't to suggest there's anything wrong with boarding the 'fast and more' train. On the contrary, it's a way of life for most people and probably the catalyst that brought us here today. The irony of the briefcase is that it's a burden to begin with but later serves as a blessing towards our journey inward. The journey of the briefcase is the journey that most people have to take in order to open their eyes and see things, as if for the very first time."

I could tell the businessman was confused, just as I had been before, and curious to understand what he meant by "inward."

"The circle of life, as I see it, begins with chasing outward treasures. Most of us embark on the 'fast and more' train because that's what we're programmed to do and believe. We think it's the right thing to do and the only path that ensures a degree of financial security and success. Along the way we earn our diplomas, collect our certificates and titles hoping they'll be tickets to a better life. To a certain extent they are, but at what price? Our professions end up defining and marking us for life. It's confining. Imagine how difficult it is for doctors and lawyers to reinvent themselves.

"At some point along the way we begin to question and reevaluate our choices. It can be sparked by a painful event that brings into question our path and even our very own existence. This prompts a spiritual shift as we try to make sense of why our spouse of ten years wanted out and disease wanted in. And believe it or not, pain can actually lead to a better you. I know what you're thinking but please hear me out. Suffering's a part of life and that's a fact. It can serve as a kind of baptism for the soul. Suffering can lead to an awakening, a discovery that the greatest treasures in the world actually reside inside of us. It's abundant, infinite and called 'love.' That's why I'd call the journey we're all on an odyssey to the heart."

He turned to the businessman and asked if he could relate.

The businessman seemed completely confused but said, "Please continue."

The golden man set down the briefcase and eyed a black suitcase which belonged to one of the other passengers. I knew we were going to be treated to a live performance from a master storyteller.

"Would you like to know what humanity's purpose is?"

He grabbed the suitcase and awkwardly walked backward in a counterclockwise direction. I was worried he was going to trip and fall over and I think his wife shared the same sentiment.

"Walking backwards, in a way, is a metaphor for moving inward toward our spiritual center. In our world, as you know, moving forward is considered progress, while moving backwards is regarded as a weakness or setback. In reality, however, personal and professional setbacks can be an impetus to spiritual growth.

"But where does the journey lead?" asked the businessman.

"That, my dear friend, is the million-dollar question and I have the billion-dollar answer!"

We laughed.

"Each loss, each failure, each dark moment brings us a step closer to salvation and to the core of who we really are. As my wife can attest, I usually ask people whom I meet for the first time to tell me who they are. I pause, and then ask them to tell me who they *really* are. At first, they're confused but the reason I ask again is because most of us lose touch with our true selves along the way. I doubt who you are today is an accurate reflection of who you were not long ago. Remember the masks we used to wear, especially the ones that camouflaged us with the identities of our profession?"

We nodded.

"The beauty of the universe is that it begins to work its magic as we begin to lose our outer way. Hardships push some people to the brink of despair and others to travel inwardly to a place I call home. I'll elaborate. Just as I started walking backwards from this point, notice how I ended up returning to the same spot. It's just like the circle of life and what it means to go back home. It's returning to the place where it all began. The journey's a natural longing, a thirst most of us have to reconnect with our eternal roots. As life progresses, over time the journey of two steps forward, one step back shifts to one step forward and two steps back.

"I carry the suitcase to illustrate that, sooner or later, we're called to pack our bags and head back home. Not home as a place where we grew up but an imaginary place within ourselves. As I mentioned, it's a spiritual journey and one we can only take if we're ready to answer the calling. At some point along this inward journey, step by step, year by year, we come face to face with our heart and soul. 'Welcome back home!' say the heart and soul. 'Where have you been all this time?'

"Of course, not everybody connects but it's a divine moment for those who do. This is an odyssey to the heart, the point when a spiritual awakening occurs and your life's purpose is revealed. When it happens, a gush of love and joy emanates from you and back to you, in a constant loop that never ends. Your heart explodes with unconditional love and gratitude as it begins to see the sacredness in everything, even in the darkest of moments.

"Our journey begins with two steps or maybe even three steps forward and one step back. As life progresses, we're confronted with situations that cause us to reconsider our path.

As a result, some of us take fewer steps forward and larger steps inward toward our center.

"The final phase of our journey consists solely of moving inward, where we discover treasures that never wane. We see this inward preference especially among people who realize they don't have a lot of time left. They seek deeper and more meaningful connections with life, which can only be found in abundance within themselves."

I couldn't believe what I was hearing. He was basically describing how I felt and including many of the things I had been journaling about, like seeing the world with our heart and not just through our eyes.

The businessman picked up his briefcase and said, "I feel like throwing this damn thing out the window."

I told him to relax and that his feelings were perfectly normal. After all, we were all there.

"I get the circle of life thing, but I want to achieve so much more. I don't feel like staying on this damn 'slow and less' train and want to get off at the next station," said the businessman.

"That's perfectly fine," said my friend. "We all go through periods of uncertainty and feel like changing tracks along the way. Just keep in mind that there's no wrong place to be in life as long as you accept there's a reason for where you're supposed to be. If you can be at peace with that, it changes everything."

I think the businessman, like myself, was intrigued by it all.

He asked the golden man one last question. "With so much life experience, what other advice could you give us?"

"Invest in real estate," smirked the golden man.

I was surprised. Of all people, I didn't expect him to say that.

The businessman was also surprised and wanted to make sure he heard the same thing. The businessman repeated, "Invest in real estate?"

"Yes, invest in real estate," confirmed the golden man.

"But a lot of my friends have bought property only to see the value of their investments evaporate. They're hugely indebted," he said.

"What I mean is to invest in the valuable real estate that

resides between your left and right ear." He tapped the top of his head to point out where. "This land," he said, "is the most valuable investment you'll ever make. It's an investment in you. It yields constant dividends for the rest of your life and, as a businessman, I'm sure you're familiar with the term 'return on investment.'"

"Of course," said the businessman.

"Well, the return on investment on your education and personal development can't be measured. It's priceless. It will never lose value over time and you can take it with you wherever you go and use it whenever you want. Unlike property, knowledge can't be seized or taken away from you for failing to meet your loan obligations. So keep learning and keep growing."

Eleven

The Hunter

I don't know what happened next because, when I looked around, there was no sign of the golden couple or the businessman. Again, I must have fallen asleep, something I didn't do much for fear of falling behind in my career. I looked out of the train window hoping to catch a glimpse of my friends. Instead, I witnessed a wave of people rushing to get on board while others disembarked.

Suddenly I heard a tap on the window. It was the businessman.

"We didn't want to wake you up," he said as he waved goodbye and disappeared into the masses of fellow commuters.

I was confused. I didn't know how I had lost sight of them but realized that a lot of people enter our lives and leave; some we notice and others we don't. Some leave a lasting impression while others play a role that only becomes clearer later in life. I hadn't been aware of this before but I realized every person could be a teacher. I had a feeling I'd meet the golden couple again and, even if I didn't, I felt grateful for the brief time we had spent together.

This time, a well-built man entered the compartment. He had an untamed beard that dropped below his neck and wore camouflage pants with brown boots.

"Howdy," he said as he made his way toward an empty seat.

I acknowledged his entry and told him he was welcome. I didn't know what to make of him and refrained from drawing any inferences about who he was or what he did.

"I know what you're thinking," said the man in a husky voice. "You couldn't take your eyes off my dirty boots and probably drew conclusions about who I was and what I do for a living."

"I'm sorry," I said, "I didn't realize I was staring at your boots."

"Just kidding," he said. "Take a look at me from head to toe and tell me what goes through your mind."

He seemed to be a playful character, so I obliged. "Judging by your camouflage clothes, green cap and boots, you could be a construction worker, farmer, soldier or hunter. I doubt you're a soldier because they wouldn't let you grow a beard so I'll go with recreational hunter."

"Good guess. Ex-hunter, actually," he said. "My father and grandfather were hunters. Ever since I was a young child, they'd take me hunting with them. I was too young to carry a heavy rifle. I think I was around eight when I first pulled the trigger. I knew my dad was damn proud of me because he'd often boast to his friends that I had a good eye and was always the first to spot hare and quail. The hunting season was the best time of the year. It meant packing our bags with snacks and ammo. I enjoyed pulling the trigger under my dad's supervision and it didn't matter if I shot anything or not.

"As I grew older and more experienced, hunting evolved from the thrill of shooting for the sake of it to the thrill of who could return home with the most game. Hunting was a sport. It became a competition, a numbers game to see who could bring home the most kills and boast the biggest story. We'd compete for bragging rights and exaggerate about the one that got away. The feeling of being out in nature with our friends and toys was fun and exciting. It was a temporary escape from bills and bosses. Along the way, I got married and started a family.

"I continued to hunt but it wasn't as much fun as it used to be. Things started changing. My daughter thought that hunters were cruel people. I tried to explain to her that it was part of our family tradition, passed on from one generation to the next. She wasn't convinced. She had an unusually high empathy for all animals but, it seemed, even more for the ones I'd bring home than the ones she'd occasionally eat. I remember how she cried and went to her bedroom one time when I brought a mother hare back home. I had been looking forward to having a nice dinner but something felt different that time. I knocked on her door and entered her bedroom.

"She said, 'Daddy, this is for you.'

"She handed me a card in the shape of a heart. The top part of the heart was sketched to resemble slightly exaggerated ears and just below them were eyes shedding a stream of tears. I think she was depicting a mother hare. At the bottom of the heart, she wrote, 'Love mommies.'

"I continued to hunt but not as often. I'd go mostly to enjoy the experience of being outdoors and to burn some calories. My appreciation of nature and animals grew deeper. I'd spend less time aiming at birds and hares along the barrel of a rifle and more time just observing how beautiful they were when roaming freely in their natural habitat. I'd spend hours walking aimlessly down dirt tracks and return home physically exhausted but totally rejuvenated inside. I'd sit under evergreen trees and talk openly about my problems with my dog. She seemed to be the only one who'd listen. It was a natural type of therapy from the chaos of life in the big city. It was so beneficial that I often wondered why doctors couldn't prescribe the outdoors as a form of medication to their patients. Nature can cure a lot of problems, especially the imaginary ones.

"Then something unbelievable happened. I went hunting alone, without my friends and two dogs. I took a nap around noon time and I woke up to feel something licking my face. It was the largest deer I had ever seen. If I took her home, I'd earn bragging rights for the rest of my life. It was surreal. My rifle was loaded and leaning against the tree beside me. She looked into my eyes and rubbed her ears against my beard. Nobody would believe this story. For a split second, I thought of my daughters' card. I didn't react. I just looked straight back into the deer's eyes and felt an immense kinship as if we had been friends forever. I never considered myself as a spiritual person but that moment was sacred and will remain imprinted in my soul forever.

"On my way home, I reflected on the incident. I tried to make sense of that rarest of rare encounters. Was it just a dream or did it really happen? How could I explain it to my friends without them making fun of me and thinking I was a liar? I've heard of out-of-body experiences and wondered if that's what it was. I felt as if my body had momentarily entered the deer's and then I peered back at myself from the perspective of the deer.

"A stream of tears rolled down my cheeks, just like the ones my daughter had drawn on the card. It was a strange feeling, almost impossible to describe. I felt I wasn't separate from the deer but joined to it by an intelligence higher than I could fathom. I've heard some people describe it as a state of oneness, an abstract concept I couldn't relate to until that fateful day years ago. I think it boils down to being kind and compassionate, which is something that ferments in all of us to one degree or another, until it reveals itself as oneness.

"I couldn't stop thinking about what happened, but I was hungry and since I hadn't killed dinner, I thought I'd buy it. I stopped by a grocery store and the guy in front of me placed a skinned rabbit on the conveyor belt. It was intact from head to tail. I felt a strange feeling inside. It was the first time I was seeing a rabbit, not as food but as a living entity that had the same right to life as I did. When I got home, I could tell that my daughter was relieved to see I had returned empty-handed. She pumped her fist into the air as a sign of victory. My wife walked up to me and took a suspicious look at my beard.

"'What's up with your beard,' she asked. 'Looks like you polished it with gel or something.'

"That's when I knew the encounter with the deer hadn't been a dream but something that actually happened. That was the day I decided to give up hunting."

"Sorry for rambling on," he said, turning to me. "I asked you to guess who I was and instead I went on and on about hunting."

I told him there was no need to apologize for sharing such a beautiful and meaningful story.

"That's a cool-looking notebook," he said.

"Thanks, it's magical too," I said proudly, pointing to the cover and asking him to tell me what he saw without blinking his eye.

He instantly saw the eye become a sun and said, "That's crazy cool!"

He observed that I had been taking notes while he spoke about hunting and wondered curiously what I was journaling about.

"Did you write that I was an evil man who enjoyed killing animals but later found redemption?" he asked with a smile.

I chuckled and said I'd left the 'evil' part out. I then told him about a fisherman I had met who increasingly felt discomfort when seeing the fish he had caught gasp and flop on the deck of his fishing boat.

"I can believe that," said the ex-hunter. "I've seen grown men and women cry when trees were cut down. I'll never forget the outrage of a woman I met. Her words still ring in my head. She said, 'How can they justify murdering such glorious trees that once provided shade to five generations and shelter to thousands of nesting birds.'

"She said it was heartbreaking to see them chainsaw sacred trees for the sake of profit. Cutting trunks felt like they were cutting her legs. 'It was painful,' she said. That's the feeling of being completely part of something, seeing the whole rather than parts, the oneness we were talking about."

A young lady sitting across from me, who had joined us earlier and was listening in on our conversation, added, "We're all guilty. We claim to like flowers but only a few of us really love them."

"What do you mean?" I asked.

"Well, I'm sure you've heard it before but it's worth repeating. Those who like flowers selfishly pick them to give to people they love on special occasions or use them to adorn kitchen tables. But people who really love flowers have no urge to pick them. They leave them intact so they can be enjoyed by others, including the bees."

This got me thinking. Did I love flowers or just like them? I think I fell in the middle, but the scale was swiftly tipping toward love, as with all things in my life. After listening to stories about hunters, fishermen and nature lovers, I began to recognize oneness more often. It wasn't just something I understood conceptually. I had begun feeling it on a much deeper level. I turned to an empty page of my journal and tried to explain oneness based on the stories I had heard and on my own experiences. I began to write that oneness was seeing yourself in all of life, an awareness that extended far beyond just feeling connected to a deer or a tree; but more so, as if we were the deer or the tree. A bullet to the deer is a bullet to your gut. An axe to a branch is an axe to your leg. What you do to them, you do to yourself. There's no distinction or distance between you and them. Whatever you are, they are, and whatever they are, you are.

I looked out of the window and reflected more on the idea of oneness. It became clear that many of the things I had once regarded as distant or separate from who I was now resided in my heart. I felt closer to and more intimate with the wonders of the universe. I began rationalizing that, if people, plants and animals lived inside me, I couldn't consider them as a separate entity from who I was. I wondered how I could articulate this more clearly if asked to explain it.

It was dark outside and I could see a galaxy of stars. That's when I remembered the majestic image of planet Earth as viewed from space. It was an unforgettable image engraved in my head as a curious teenager lost in the pages of science and geography magazines. The idea became just as clear as the image: billions of people, divided by beliefs, yet bound together as humans, inhabiting a place they call home. I mused at the idea of how oneness, no separation of one from the other, could render wars obsolete. I marveled at the remote possibility of harmonious coexistence, just as appeared from space. It has to be possible, I thought. After all, doesn't humanity have humanity in common? Isn't love a universal feeling, not bound by time, space or form? And that's when it occurred to me what it meant to be unified, together as one. Fortunately, we don't have to travel into space to experience this type of union or connection; it resides in each and every one of us and its base camp is the heart, a place we call home, and a state of being that we call "love."

The hunter-turned-conservationist stood up and extended his hand. He gave me a firm handshake and said, "Love you, bro."

I was taken aback. Three words that meant so much. Despite having only met him just a few hours earlier, I felt as if we had been friends since childhood, maybe even before that. He was one of those rare individuals you come across and connect with instantly. I never used to believe in soulmates but all of that changed since I boarded the 'slow and less' train. I suppose I'm now more open to the possibility that soulmates may exist.

I gave him a warm hug and said, "Thanks, buddy."

I knew his daughter had changed his life with a moving note she had left for him when he came back from hunting one day. I wanted to recognize her for what she did, so I decided to forward a precious gift that had been given to me. It wasn't a difficult decision. I gave him my bookmark, the one my friend's daughter had drawn, with the help of the golden lady. I explained the story behind the bookmark and he was moved by my gesture. He promised he'd give it to his daughter and off he went.

Twelve

Music of the Heart

I thought of all the wonderful people I had met on this journey and how I had learned so many things from the stories they shared. Each story was unique and contained a common message. All of them had experienced some sort of crisis in their lives, something painful or severely unpleasant that had led to a shift in consciousness. It's as if suffering had been a prerequisite for opening the doors of their hearts. I tried to understand this better and thought how pain probably chips away at the ego until it no longer has the strength or stamina to defend itself. It seems that the gradual breakdown of the ego eventually gives birth to a new way of looking at life, a heightened awareness.

It occurred to me that a lot of the pain we experience is actually self-inflicted and caused primarily by our thoughts. I began to understand that what we feel and how we react depends largely on our interpretation and perception of the external environment. If, however, our perceptions of events are filtered through the lens of love and compassion rather than the destructive lens of the mind and ego, life becomes much more pleasurable. I wrote these observations in my journal and added: "If you feel love, you'll see love in everything and everyone."

Just as I had completed that sentence, a young woman entered the compartment. She wore white trainers, tight black leggings and a short-sleeved T-shirt that read "I love life." She also wore a pink running cap with a heart on the front and hole at the back to allow for her chestnut hair to be tied into a ponytail. She seemed to be in her early thirties, confident and independent. She lugged a guitar case on her slim frame but what struck me was that she entered tapping a thin white cane on the floor with one hand while holding a short dog leash in the other. Her best friend was a guide dog, a well-trained Labrador.

I was impressed. She appeared to be visually impaired or maybe even blind but that didn't diminish her mobility or adventurous travel spirit. I was quick to tell her there was plenty of room and asked her if I could help her unload her backpack.

"Yes, thanks!" She said. "You sound like a gentleman. They're rare nowadays. Do you mind if I sit next to you?" she asked.

"Of course not," I said, as I proceeded to remove her backpack and assist her in settling into her seat.

The Labrador looked up at me suspiciously but gave me the benefit of the doubt.

For some reason, I was feeling nervous and noticed my heart beating a little faster. I knew I was sitting next to someone special. We didn't exchange words for what seemed like an eternity. This surprised me because I didn't consider myself particularly shy in social settings.

I finally mustered the courage to say, "Excuse me, what's the name of your dog?"

She grinned. "This is Joy," she said as she leaned over to stroke Joy's head.

Joy seemed to understand she was being introduced and tilted her head at me. I held out my hand and she licked it, as if to say, "Pleased to meet you!"

The woman, seeming to sense the interaction, giggled and said, "A friend of Joy's is a friend of mine. Sometimes we connect with animals first and people second, or people first and animals second. It makes no difference. We're all the same."

That was beautiful and I asked her if I could write that down in my notepad.

"Oh, so you're a writer?" she asked inquisitively.

"Perhaps an aspiring one but for now I'm just an observer of life."

She laughed and tapped the side of her head with her index finger.

"Oh, I see, so you're one of those deep thinker types, a philosopher right? Don't people like you end up poor and on the streets?" she said teasingly and added, "Life's to be lived and not understood."

She had a great sense of humor and her energy was contagious. She made it so easy to be likable, especially since she was awash in lavender, my favorite scent. I was just about to compliment her when she said, "I think you like the smell of my perfume, don't you?"

"Absolutely. How did you know that?" I asked curiously.

"Maybe it's because over the years I've acquired a kind of sixth sense, especially after losing my eyesight when I was twelve years old. I'm more aware of sounds. I heard you breathing deeply through your nose, you took a couple of whiffs like people do when smelling roses."

I blurted out, "You're amazing."

"And you're good for my health," she replied without missing a beat.

"What do you mean?" I asked.

She laughed and said, "I thought you were the academic type who knew everything. Don't you know that being around good people is also good for your health."

"And what about the not-so-good ones?" I asked.

"They're just as good but in a different way. Bad apples, like bad people, have their purpose too. Their unconscious behavior serves as teachings for our spiritual growth, just like working out in a gym. Muscles only grow and get stronger after being stressed by lifting weights. There's an adage for it: 'No pain, no gain.'

"People are like weights," she continued. "They can strengthen our spiritual muscles, by silencing our urge to judge and criticize others. They can teach us to be patient, more tolerant and accept others as they are and not how we want them to be. It doesn't mean we condone their behavior. It's just that reacting, instead of observing without judgement, can exacerbate the situation and be detrimental to our health."

I was impressed by her attitude to life. Good experiences feed the heart and soul and bad ones somehow fuel our spiritual development. I knew this lovely woman was wise beyond her years. I wondered if losing her eyesight at the age of twelve had played a role in her world outlook and thought about how the obstacles she had overcome had probably made her into the gem she was today.

"Hold my hand and place it directly over your heart," she said. Her request caught me off guard, but I obliged.

"What's your heart so afraid of and why is it beating so fast? It's beating as fast as when I go out on brisk walks with Joy."

I was at a loss for words and embarrassed to confess that I had "butterfly" feelings for her.

"You really like me, don't you?" she asked with a smile only an angel could make.

I wasn't comfortable telling her how I felt just yet, so I didn't say a thing.

"Do you know how I can order something to drink?" she asked.

I pressed the service bell and told her someone would be here to take her order shortly.

"So, Mr. Observer of life, what else have you figured out about me?" she asked playfully.

I told her she had an amazing sense of humor.

She wasn't impressed and said, "Come on philosopher, you can do better than that. How on earth do you expect to write a bestseller?"

I caved. "It's difficult to describe. You're unique. There's something special about you. You have this soothing presence, a magnetic aura that's rarely found in others. It's hard to put into words but the first things I noticed about you were your floral aroma, your heart-symbol hat and shirt, and your independent spirit."

"Ah, now you're talking! Please continue and it had better be worthy of a bestseller," she added jokingly.

I had to remind her that I was just an observer of life, taking notes. I asked her if she could tell me about the heart on her hat and the "I love life" written on her shirt. The word "love" appeared in the shape of a pink heart.

She chuckled. "The heart on my hat and shirt is a reminder of everything I am today. Joy is my best friend and I gave her that name because I began feeling happy only after I started listening to my heart. My father was a mathematician, a thinker like you, so I grew up believing that science had all the answers to our burning questions. He'd complain to my mother that his children weren't using their heads often enough. He once told us that God gave us brains to use, and for him that meant analyzing everything and crunching numbers. I remember he'd plan trips and make purchasing decisions based on the variables he'd plug into his mathematical mind. Being raised by a father like that meant most of our decisions were governed by logic. I paid the price for adopting that limited belief.

"Let me explain," she went on.

"My ex-husband was a successful investment banker. We owned multiple homes and cars and often travelled to exotic destinations. But there was a problem: my heart wasn't committed to the man I had married for all the wrong reasons. I suffered in silence for too many years and my heart pleaded for freedom. I remember one night we had a huge argument about money. I was furious. I slammed the door on my husband and ran out into the yard.

"I was so upset and sobbed uncontrollably. Here I was, with every material trapping anybody could ever dream of having, yet my heart was totally broken. That's when I had an epiphany. Tears were rolling down my cheeks but then I started laughing at the absurdity of it all. I realized we possess two minds, a mind of the mind, and a mind of the heart. The mind of the heart works just like intuition: it understands things without needing proof or evidence. I knew which mind I had used when

I had decided to get married. It was the mind which prioritized financial security. It struck me that most of the decisions I had made in life relied on the mind of my mind and not the mind of my heart. I think this explained why I had been unhappy for a good part of my life.

"As an aspiring artist, I was a right-brain thinker trying to live in a left-brain world. I remember reading a book that explained how right-brain thinkers relied mostly on imagination and intuition. They saw the world through a lens of artistic images and colors while left-brain thinkers were methodical, analytical and thought in words and numbers. That's when I got this sinking feeling that, for way too long, I had been denying my natural right-brain tendencies.

"It was the breakthrough I needed to exit my failed marriage. I began relying more on my intuition and making consensual decisions with my heart. Of course, I relied on my left brain to help but just not as much. It was difficult in the beginning because it contradicted all my dad's teachings.

"But things began to change. The more I followed my heart, the more I noticed I was happier. Friends noticed I had more energy and looked happier. They said I smiled and laughed more. They were right. I kept following my heart until one day it led me to the doorstep of an internationally renowned guitarist. He believed in me when I didn't believe in myself. He encouraged me to take guitar lessons. At first, I thought it would be an impossible task given my visual impairment but I was wrong. Even though I couldn't see the strings, I had a knack for hitting the right chords at the right time. News spread quickly that I was a blind guitarist with amazing vocals. I made headlines in the local paper and then it got picked up by national news outlets. They described me using words like 'prodigy,' 'gifted,' and 'outrageously talented,' but it just felt like I was doing what I was always meant to do. One thing led to another and now I perform solo across the country. It was life-changing, a decision based on my heart and not my mind. No amount of logic would have suggested I take up guitar lessons or explained my last-minute decision to embark on this trip without giving it a second thought.

"This doesn't mean I don't use my brains anymore; it's just that I also pay attention to my heart. So the advice I have for you and my dad back home is to bet a chunk of your chips on the heart and not just rely on the mind to make decisions. Sometimes love trumps logic. It always does."

***

"Our turtle girl just arrived," I said, trying to be a little funny with my guitar star friend. I explained how the uniforms of those who worked on the train had images of cute little turtles as a reference to the slow train we were on.

She smiled.

"How can I help?" asked a service attendant who had appeared at our table.

My friend ordered some green tea and asked the attendant if she had any matches. The attendant reminded her that smoking was prohibited on the train.

"Sweetie, who said I wanted to smoke? I'd just like to light my sacred little candle, it's one I travel with everywhere I go."

The attendant apologized for assuming she was going to smoke and said she would allow her to light the candle provided it was placed securely on the table. A gentleman sitting across from us reached out to offer his cigarette lighter. I thanked him and lit my friend's scented red candle.

We ordered our drinks and everyone in the compartment, including Joy, sat staring at the candle as if we were a tribe bonding around a well-lit campfire. I had been a Scout but it had never occurred to me that a tiny flicker from a candle could create an ambience of camaraderie among strangers. I knew my friend was special but now I was convinced she was divine. How else could I explain a blind woman wanting to light a candle whose flicker she'd never see? I wanted to understand what was going through her mind. I think everybody else in the compartment was just as curious about the significance of the candle. I was ready to ask but she beat me to it.

"Hey everybody, what do you think of the candle?" she asked.

I was the first to thank her and tell her how soothing the candle looked on the table.

"I know, you're probably wondering why a blind person like me would carry a candle around? I get asked that question a lot. Interested in knowing why?"

"Yes," we said in unison.

"Well, it all began when I was a little girl. I loved helping my mother make candles in our kitchen during the holidays. We'd make them in various shapes, colors and sizes. We'd melt wax and then pour them into hollow molds. Some were cylindrical and others shaped like Christmas trees, hearts stars, or – my favorite – owls. It was a ritual my mother and I enjoyed every year. It added to the Christmas spirit just as much as her freshly baked ginger cookies did. We'd make as many as twenty to thirty candles. Some were used to decorate our home, and the rest to give out as Christmas gifts. I often asked my mother who the candles were for and I'd never get a straight answer. The candles were given as gifts to families I didn't even know.

I could tell some of the families were struggling and a few lived alone, as if abandoned by the world.

"My mother passed away when I was twenty but her candles, lessons and light will live on forever. In fact, I can feel her presence right now. Can you?" she asked us.

We said we could and continued listening to her story.

"A few years ago, a lady I didn't recognize approached me after one of my performances. She asked if I was the little candle girl who used to visit her every Christmas with my mother. I said I thought I was and that's when she began to sob. I'll never forget that moment. She apologized for getting emotional and stepped back to explain why. She told me I was probably too young to remember but credited my mother with saving her life.

"I knew my mom was a saint, just not canonized, and this was proof, yet again, of the impact she had on others.

"The lady went on to recall how my mother and I had appeared on her doorstep during the darkest period of her life. She had been an orphan and had left her adoptive family when she was just seventeen years old. Years later, she moved in with a man who turned out to be abusive. She fled and jumped from one odd job to another to make ends meet. Eventually she moved into a tiny home but still couldn't pay off the bills that piled up. She fell into despair and didn't know what to do when her landlord threatened to evict her if she didn't pay the rent by the end of the month. At one point, things got so bad she wanted to end her life. She turned to drugs and alcohol for solace. It was a way, as she said, to escape from her hopeless future and forget her day-to-day misery.

"'Your mom was a sweet soul,' the lady said to me. 'She knew everything about me and never felt compelled to judge or belittle my actions. She didn't help financially but gave me something more valuable than money could ever buy: her time and a heart-shaped candle that changed my life. I remember the three words she uttered as if it were yesterday. She said, "You're just like this candle."'

"It was probably the first time I had smiled in months. She said that we're all like candles, you, me and everybody! We're all energy, we're all light; but like candles on a windy or rainy day, our light can be extinguished by an abusive partner, financial hardship or failing health. She said that just because I was going through a difficult time didn't mean my 'life candle' would never be lit again.

"Your mother then lit a candle you were holding and asked you to light my candle with your lit candle.

"'Do you remember that?' she asked me. I didn't. She then said that after I lit her candle, she felt a deep sense of peace and hope for the future that she had not felt in ages.

"'As we held our lit candles, your mom said, 'Love is light. As long as someone cares, and there always will be someone who does, your life candle will be lit, no matter what your life circumstances are. It may go out once in a while but if you're surrounded by love, it will be lit again just as we lit your candle.'

"'Your mother taught me to believe in the power of love and to put my faith in the goodness of the universe. We're all vulnerable to the ups and downs of life but, with love, we can prevail and even learn to light our own candles.'

"So, my dear friends, that's the story of why I always carry a candle wherever I go. I light it with every opportunity I have. My mom helped countless people and I hope this candle can do the same for you."

I gazed at the flicker and then at Joy. We sat in silence. It was quiet for a while and a chance to reflect on the people I met and things I learned on the journey. I looked back at Joy. Her eyes were beaming straight back at me. I imagined playing the stare game I used to play with my sister when we were kids. We'd look into each other's eyes and try to keep them open for as long as possible without blinking. The first to blink would lose. I don't think it was ever played against a dog but then again, I contemplated the possibility that I could be playing against a person, perhaps from another life, disguised as a dog. I sensed we were equals.

About ten minutes later, the service attendant brought our drinks and I left a generous tip.

"Do you mind if we hold each other's hands?" asked my friend.

My heart was about to explode. Our hands connected and landed on my tense lap.

"Please tell me about yourself and the things you've observed about life."

I paused for a moment to collect my thoughts and take a deep breath. "Well," I said, "first of all you're an astonishing woman. You carry a candle whose flicker you can't see but the truth is you can see more than all of us. My eyes are open but not as open as yours. You're living proof that we can live a more fulfilling and meaningful life by tapping into our inner sense. We can have perfect eyesight and not see or enjoy the world as much as those who experience the world through the eyes of the heart."

I could feel her hand tighten around mine when she said, "I like how that came out and would love if you could help me write a song."

She asked me if I could help remove her guitar from its case. I had a good feeling our ears were in for a treat. My heart, and I'm sure everybody else's in the compartment, was begging for her to play the guitar. Joy barked, approvingly I hope, as I removed the guitar from its protective case and handed it over to its gifted owner.

She spent a minute fine tuning the strings and said she'd dedicate the song to me.

I was flattered.

She began running her fingers up and down the strings and then said, "I don't have to see you to know you're one of a kind; I can feel it."

I was at a loss for words. She began to play the guitar and sing with angelic vocals, the kind that give you goosebumps:

Migrants of life, aren't we all?
Drifting, displaced in search of it all
Where is it? What is it?
I wanna know. I gotta go.
Oh babe, it ain't so.
It's here in a song.
It's love. It's light
It's bright and in sight.
Babe, go home
You won't be alone.
You've got the keys.
You are the keys
It's the greatest art, go to your heart.
Love is the way
Light is the way
Migrants of life, aren't we all?
Babe, babe
It's the greatest art, go to your heart.

I froze in disbelief. Her impromptu song, coupled with her breathtaking vocals, encapsulated the very essence of what I had felt and learned on this new path I had consciously chosen. The train came to a stop and so did my heart. Joy and my new friend were about to disembark. As we embraced, I wondered if we'd ever meet again. She said, "I know what you're thinking, and the answer is yes, we will."

***

I was in a pensive mood; sad, yet strangely hopeful. The train departed and I couldn't recall the name of the last stop or where we were heading. I was fine with not knowing. Sometimes you're the driver and sometimes you're the passenger. That's how life works and the sooner you accept that, the more comfortable your ride will be.

I began to understand how the metaphor of driving versus being a passenger applied to my life. It made perfect sense. Passengers get to see and experience things that would be impossible to notice if they were driving. A passenger has a completely different view than a driver has, even though they share they the same path and destination. If I had been on the 'fast and more' train, I doubt that I'd have had the time or patience to talk with the amazing people I had met on the 'slow and less' train. Of course, they wouldn't have been on the same train. I had learned so much from the intimate stories that they had shared, and which I had recorded in my journal.

Each page, and there were hundreds, provided a glimpse, a hidden gem, of how best to live life. I picked up my journal and began to skim through the pages. I began reliving many of the stories, including those of the businessman, the golden couple, the rock star and the blind guitarist. They were inspiring and all had one thing in common. I wrote, "If every word in this journal could slide off the pages like a grain of sand, it would spell 'LOVE.'" Despite my uncertainty, for the first time I began feeling more comfortable with the idea of not knowing what the future held in store for me.

Thirteen

Arriving at the Heart

I can't say how long the final leg of my journey was. It felt like a lifetime. Perhaps it was.

I got off at the next stop and ventured out into the city.

I purchased some snacks from the kiosk and the cash register clerk put both of her hands in front of her mouth, as a gesture of disbelief, and said, "You won't believe this. It's your lucky day."

I smiled to be polite but wasn't sure what she meant.

She said, "You have to play the lottery."

I was confused and asked her why.

She said, "I've been working at this cash register for almost three years and never issued an unusual receipt like yours. It contains nothing but ones on it."

I was tempted to try my luck, especially with the encouragement of the charming clerk cheering me on and knowing that the stop I had got off at was number eleven. Instead of purchasing a lottery ticket, I decided I'd spend the loose change on a hot cup of coffee. I walked for a few blocks and to my delight, discovered a cozy-looking café with a lot of people sitting outside.

There was a huge line of people waiting to get in. I guessed it would take at least twenty minutes to be seated, but I wasn't in a rush, at least not anymore. I asked the gentleman in front of me if he knew anything about the place.

"Yes, this is my favorite place to relax and people watch."

I smiled and remembered the words of my uncle who had traveled extensively around the world. He'd always say, "Trust the locals, they know best."

I wanted to sit outside and people-watch too but all tables were occupied. Suddenly I heard someone call out my name. I couldn't believe it. It was the golden-couple lady with the long silver hair. She was thrilled to see me just as much as I was to see her.

"He's with me," she told the hostess at the entrance of the bistro.

She grabbed my hand and led me to the table where she was sitting. We had a perfect view of a narrow cobblestone street in the old part of town. Hundreds of tourists walked by, delighted by the picturesque surroundings. I turned my head toward the hostess and noticed a long line of people anxious to be seated. I felt sorry for them. They were probably wondering how lucky I was for slipping through without having to wait a minute in line. We sat down and ordered some coffee. I told her how beautiful her long silver hair looked, just as I had remembered it awhile back.

"And how's your wise other half?" I asked.

"He passed away," she said.

I gave her my condolences and told her he had left a lasting impression on me.

"Our encounter on the train years ago was brief," I said, "but your husband taught me so many things about life, especially how to live it."

She closed her eyes and took a deep breath.

"I can feel him," she said, "He's here and happy to see us together. He suffered a stroke but lived life knowing it could happen to him any day. High blood pressure ran like a river through his family."

I understood exactly what she meant about feeling his presence. I did too. After all, she's the one who believed we change forms, just as sugar does when added to coffee. I remember taking notes that reflected her views on mortality and how she thought we never died but dissolved our way into eternity.

She asked me if I still enjoyed writing and if I had ever published the book that was a dream years ago. I told her I had amassed plenty of notes but not enough confidence to turn them into a book. As a writer who had once struggled to impress his English teacher in middle school, I still had reservations and self-doubt to overcome.

"Don't worry and never second-guess yourself," she said. "Everything will be all right. My late husband imparted pearls of wisdom during the last few months of his life. You've got to include them in your book and get it published."

My ears were wide open as I pulled out my journal and prepared to take some notes. Life was good. We were enjoying each other's company and I told her how blessed I felt for bumping into her.

"It was meant to be," she said.

That's when our coffee arrived. I couldn't believe she still remembered that I drank black coffee with a heap of sugar and no cream. She opened a sachet of sugar and offered to pour it into my cup. Just as she had done on the train, she told me to pay close attention to how sugar dissolves in coffee. I thanked her as I took my first sip. She then asked me to look straight into the cup and tell her what I saw.

I leaned over the cup and saw the silhouette of my head on the surface of the coffee. It reminded me of other reflections, like the one I had seen in the pond and in the train window. They were "aha" moments that had illuminated my understanding of life as being a reflection of what we feel inside. This time, I looked at my reflection in the coffee and felt the strange sensation that her husband was looking back at me. It was bizarre.

I shared my feelings with her, and she smiled.

"Of course it's him," she said. "Since we both feel his presence inside us, we can see him too."

It totally clicked: the idea that the world we see is based on the world we feel inside. I was overwhelmed with emotion and promised her that I'd begin to write the book. I felt compelled and responsible to honor her remarkable husband. It was also a way for me to give something back to his wife for teaching me so much, not just now but when we had first met on the 'slow and less' train.

A little sparrow landed on our table for a moment and just looked at me for a split second before it flitted off. The sparkle in its eye seemed so similar to my friend's.

She smiled, took another sip of coffee, and began to speak again. "Let me tell you a few things I learned before the man of my life passed away. Gratitude always played an important role in his life but he took it to extremes. I've never met anyone as grateful as my husband. He didn't thank only people – he thanked every being and object he came into contact with. He'd pet a dog and thank it for being selfless with its love. He wondered why people couldn't be more like dogs. He'd return from a day out cycling with his friends and then run his fingers across the frame of his bicycle as if it were a pet cat. I used to tease him that his bike was getting more affection than I was! He'd spend time in our backyard and I'd watch him from our kitchen window. I often heard him say, 'Thank you. Thank you. Thank you.'

"When he'd step back into the kitchen, I'd ask him what he was grateful for and he'd just say, 'For being alive.' I could see he was thirsty and offered him a glass of water. He'd say, 'It's all in here. If only everybody could see that what they're looking for can be found in their own backyard or in a glass of water.'

"He'd point to the ceiling of our kitchen and say, 'All they have to do is look up and see that they have a roof.'

"Then he'd point to his shoes and say, 'All they have to do is look down.'

"Once he arrived home waving a parking ticket in his hand. Most people would be extremely irritated and upset having received a fine but he just grinned and asked me to take a picture of him kissing the ticket. I thought he was losing his mind! He wasn't. He printed the picture and below it typed, 'Kiss-a-parking-ticket life philosophy.'

"He asked if he could place the picture on the refrigerator and I reluctantly agreed. It turned out to be a daily reminder not to allow petty things such as parking violations to ruin our entire day. I'd often think of the photo as a quick reminder to let go of things that weren't worth occupying my head for much longer than they deserved.

"There were so many life lessons like that and I felt fortunate to witness them from a man who was also my life partner. He often wondered why everybody was busy chasing something that was impermanent when all they had to do was look inside and connect with something immortal, their hearts. He was adamant about the heart emanating and reverberating love around the world long after we are gone. He believed it passes on from one generation to another and that's why he considered it eternal. He said it's so obvious and couldn't understand why anybody would be skeptical about it.

"'We had proof,' he said. 'The heart's universal language is love and just like languages, it can be taught and passed on from one generation to another.'

"Indeed, he was right. His mother passed away decades ago. She was a living saint and exemplified what it meant to live with a heart filled with love, kindness and compassion. Her acts of kindness rubbed off on my husband, our children and grandchildren.

"As my husband said, 'Why would anybody find it inconceivable to think of love as a light that never goes out, an energy that affects anybody who comes in contact with it?'

"He said it was like the Olympic torch, a flame handed from one generation to another, a transfer of energy that's immortal even after the flame goes out. I'll never forget when he said, 'Our physical body ages but our love is timeless.'

"The biggie came one day when he asked me if I ever realized we were privileged guests on planet Earth, temporary residents invited to inhabit and participate in the game of life. I couldn't quite understand what he meant by that. It sounded so esoteric until he framed it differently.

"He said, 'What do people tell their loved ones at airports

prior to their departure?'

"I said, 'They embrace and say goodbye. And perhaps, if they are like our children and grandchildren who visit during the holidays, they thank them for their hospitality too.'

"'Exactly,' he said.

"He wondered why people couldn't see that, at the end of the day, we're simply passing tourists visiting earth and, because of that, we should be prepared to depart without fear or hesitation.

"He said, 'Life should be lived as one long farewell, constantly saying goodbye to our loved ones, just like people do at airports.'

"Bingo. It's as if he was preparing for his departure all his life and being aware of it allowed him to live fully. He often said he caught glimpses of his immortality and told everybody, including you, not to fear the end of life as we know it.

"Or, in his words, 'We're just passing by.'

"Friends of ours thought he was losing his mind when he ordered a custom-made floor mat with the Latin words *memento mori*. They'd ask what it meant and laughed uneasily when he said it translated to, 'Remember that we are going to die.'

"They thought it was a strange way to welcome someone; but he was onto something because every time we entered or left our home, the mat served as a reminder that life was indeed brief and knowing so enriched ours."

My friend offered to pay and invited me to join her for a stroll along the streets of the old town. I thought it was a great idea and off we went to explore the wonderful sights and sounds of the town center. We walked past street artists and countless stores selling an array of souvenirs, snacks and just about anything you could imagine. Couples, both young and old, held hands. Live music could be heard playing in the background. It sounded familiar.

We arrived at an open square, in the center of which was a magnificent water fountain that consisted of a marble dolphin gushing water out of its mouth. People stopped to have their pictures taken in front of the inspiring sculpture. We continued to walk for a few more minutes until we came across two clowns. One sold colorful balloons and flowers while the other did face painting on a child.

I turned to my friend and asked if she felt like a tourist, enthusiastically exploring the narrow, cobbled streets of the old town.

"Of course I feel like a tourist. Aren't we all?" she said.

I nodded and said I felt the same way.

But I was curious about the music that was playing in the background. I asked her if we could walk towards the musician. She thought it was a great idea. The closer we got, the faster my heart began to beat. I could barely hear the lyrics but they sounded like the ones the blind guitarist had played for us on the train. I couldn't remember the whole song but I recognized parts of it, like, "It's the greatest art, go to your heart" and "migrants of life, aren't we all, drifting, displaced in search of it all."

There was a huge crowd blocking our view of the guitarist. We managed to squeeze our way through to the front of the group. I froze in disappointment. It wasn't the blind girl I had met on the train and dreamed of meeting again one day.

I approached the singer after she had finished performing and asked her if she knew about my star guitarist friend.

"Yes, of course I know her. How can I not know my mentor, the most talented guitarist in the world? She told me how she came up with the lyrics on a train after having met someone very special. She must have been referring to you."

I smiled and realized how, even though it wasn't my friend performing the song, her positive energy and lyrics had spread through the universe like ripples across a pond.

I thanked the singer for her kind words and dropped some change into her guitar case.

She folded a piece of paper and handed it over to me.

"Read this later," she said with a twinkle in her eye.

I didn't know what it was. I placed it in my pocket and would read it later on.

We left the town center and continued walking past numerous shops and a young acrobat who seemed like the happiest person around. I remembered the notes I had taken on the 'slow and less' train, which said that people were energy and positive people operated at higher frequencies. This acrobat was one of them. He waved enthusiastically and wished us a great day with the biggest smile I had ever seen.

I walked away, wondering how something so simple and natural as a stranger's smile, could make me tingle with joy. So yes, seemingly small and insignificant things do count. I knew I'd treasure the smallest things even more. They'd begin with every smile, sunset and rainbow.

A few minutes later, we approached an arched bridge that led to an open park across the river. The river was calm and the park dense with evergreen trees and wild flora.

My friend was noticeably tired but that didn't stop her from walking up to a tree and asking me if I knew what was so special about evergreen trees.

I said they tend to be tall, elegant and green all year round.

"Yes, absolutely," she said, "and they also have something in common with love."

"Something in common with love?" I repeated.

106

"Yes. Love, like an evergreen tree, is a constant all year round. Your heart shines three hundred and sixty-five days of the year no matter what the conditions are like."

"Kind of like a lighthouse," I added.

"Yes, love, like an evergreen tree, isn't affected by the seasons or the ups and downs of life. Evergreen trees are weatherproof, and love is 'life-proof.'"

"Wow." I took notes. "They're green in the summer and green in the darkest days of the winter. Love works in the same way."

I had never thought of love as being evergreen but it made perfect sense. She suggested we stop for a rest on a wooden bench located just a few steps away from the riverbank.

Our timing was impeccable. Just as we sat down, the sun began to set. We were about to witness the greatest show on Earth.

I told her how lucky I felt and how it was as if God were everywhere and in everything.

She grabbed my hand and said, "It's not luck, just as our encounter is not a coincidence. Everything you experience is a manifestation of your inner state, of what you feel inside. You attracted all of this and you wouldn't have noticed if you were feeling anything less than love and gratitude for life."

Indeed, I was overcome with emotion because everything I felt inside, I began to see around me. I remembered the wise words of the woman I met at the train station who said, "When your heart begins to see beyond the reach of your eyes, your life will change forever." I now knew what she meant.

I asked my friend if she saw what I saw.

"What do you mean?" she asked.

I pointed to the ducks and, just as I did, a butterfly landed on my index finger.

"Yes, I see the ducks and how you attracted a butterfly as if you were a magnet of love, and you are," she said with a wink.

It was true, I was beginning to witness and feel an abundance of love everywhere. The law of attraction wasn't just a theory but was operating in full swing, like a magnet, attracting the beautiful things I was feeling inside. But it was only when I was fully conscious and aware of those feelings that I began to notice that what lived inside of me also lived outside of me. What I felt, I began to manifest. I started hearing birds sing and noticing butterflies with more frequency. Why? Probably because I was beginning to fully appreciate and pay more attention to them. This deeper relationship with life, being more connected with all living things, meant that goldfish were no longer blinking, they were winking, and that pigeons in my backyard didn't flee out of fear, but took flight in a private airshow performed just for me. I didn't just love life, I was in love with life. That's how I felt and that's what I saw.

But I'm not naïve. We're confronted with endless problems. When one is resolved, another appears out of nowhere. I thought of my own problems and noticed that many of the issues I dreaded having to deal with, no longer had the same impact they used to. There was a certain kind of flow to situations that, in the past, would have been a great source of stress and anxiety.

"Aha," my golden friend said. "You've arrived."

"I arrived?" I asked curiously.

"You arrived at the heart. It was a bumpy journey, a lifelong odyssey that led you to where you are today, the heart. From now on, things will never be the same. You'll feel as if you have a tailwind helping you along the way. Problems will persist but they won't weigh you down as much as they used to."

I got what she meant. It's something that became clearer as I realized that life and our experiences are heavily shaped by the feelings we harbor inside. There was complete silence. We soaked in the beautiful surroundings. The lush green park behind us, the calm river in front of us and the old town across the river. I turned my head to the sun setting in the west and my jaw dropped in awe. It reminded me of the magical eye on the cover of my notebook, the one designed by my artist friend. The sun appeared as if it were a pupil briefly peering through the stoned arched bridge, like eyes of the universe.

The sun's rays stretched across the dimming blue sky like eyelashes. I didn't want to blink. It was a sacred sign, like so many others that had come before it. The eyes were those of my artist friend and, like love, she was immortal. I realized that people and situations transcend who and what they are in supernatural and majestic ways. They are without limits and no collection of words can describe where they go and who they become. It's beyond human language, just like the ability to describe who God is or what love is.

My wise friend turned to me and said, "Did you just witness what I saw?"

I nodded and knew she was referring to the sunset.

She said it reminded her of the eye illustration on the cover of my notebook that would change into the sun if you stared at it for a while without blinking.

"Look into my eyes, as you did many years ago," she said, "and tell me what you see this time."

I took a deep breath and closed my eyes before reopening them. I looked into her deep blue eyes, as I did years ago, and to my surprise, a teardrop rolled down the side of my right cheek.

"It's okay," she said, "you're weeping because you just realized that what you want, you already have and who you seek is you."

She was right. For the first time, I could see a bit of myself in her, the feeling of oneness that everybody had talked about on the 'slow and less' train. I caught a glimpse of my heart, a peek into my soul and beyond. I was moved because I had heard it described by so many others before me, including the wise lady with the beautiful sun hat that I had met at the train station. I couldn't relate back then but I did now. I realized that this idea of seeing yourself in others wasn't so foreign after all. Why should it be? Mothers feel the pain of their sick child as if it were their own pain. Animal lovers feel anguish when animals suffer, and nature lovers feel squeamish when they see trees and living organisms being abused. It's oneness with everything, the realization that we're a single living entity. It became obvious, more than ever before, that everything is in some way linked, united with no separation.

We didn't exchange words. There was complete stillness. I contemplated my uneven journey and wondered if others could relate to my experiences or if I was the only one who felt this way. Would my notes, and possibly book, resonate with others who felt the same way? Would it matter if they didn't? After all, I was just trying to figure things out. Aren't we all?

I dug into my pocket and pulled out the piece of paper the singer had given me earlier in the afternoon. I unfolded it and saw the impromptu lyrics of the song written by my blind musician friend. I read it slowly and repeatedly until the sun set.

Migrants of life, aren't we all?
Drifting, displaced in search of it all
Where is it? What is it?

I wanna know. I gotta go.
Oh babe, it ain't so.
It's here in a song.
It's love. It's light,
It's bright and in sight.
Babe, go home
You won't be alone.
You've got the keys.
You are the keys
It's the greatest art, go to your heart.
Love is the way
Light is the way
Migrants of life, aren't we all?
Babe, babe
It's the greatest art, go to your heart.

About the Author

Thales Panagides provides an inward journey that springs from his own diverse experiences in different cultures. Born in Ames Iowa, Thales earned an MBA and had aspirations for a lucrative career. But a trip to Brazil sent his life in a very different direction. What was meant to be a short stay turned into a ten-year odyssey. He founded Brazilian Bikinis, an innovative fashion business. In 2008, he relocated to Cyprus with his wife and two daughters and now lives on this idyllic island in the Eastern Mediterranean.

You can connect with me on:

🌐 https://www.thalespanagides.com

📘 https://www.facebook.com/ThalesPanagidesAuthor

✒ https://www.odysseytotheheart.com

Printed in Great Britain
by Amazon